Caxton in focus

Caxton in focus

THE BEGINNING OF PRINTING IN ENGLAND

Lotte Hellinga

THE BRITISH LIBRARY

Published by the British Library
Reference Division Publications
Great Russell Street
London WC1B 3DG

🕮 British Library Cataloguing in Publication Data

Hellinga, Lotte
 Caxton in focus: the beginning of printing in England.
 1. Printing – History – England
 I. Title
 686.2'0942 Z151

ISBN   0-904654-76-1 (cased)

Designed by Sebastian Carter
Set in Linotron Galliard
Typeset by King's English Typesetters Ltd, Cambridge
Printed and bound in Great Britain
at The Pitman Press, Bath

Contents

Acknowledgements

I would like to express my very grateful thanks to the following for permission to reproduce material in their care, as well as for generous assistance in obtaining it:

His Grace the Archbishop of Canterbury and the Trustees of Lambeth Palace Library	Colour Plates III, V, Fig. 41
The Dean and Chapter of Westminster Abbey	Cover illustration
Bruges, City Archive	Fig. 31
Cambridge University Library	Figs. 18, 29
Città del Vaticano, Biblioteca Apostolica Vaticana	Fig. 15
The Hague, Royal Library	Fig. 36
London, Public Record Office	Figs. 11, 40
London, Scolar Press	Fig. 49
Manchester, The John Rylands University Library	Colour Plate I
New York, The Pierpont Morgan Library	Figs. 30, 49
Oxford, Bodleian Library	Figs. 12, 25
San Marino, The Henry E. Huntington Library	Fig. 6

It is a pleasure to acknowledge once again my debt of gratitude to the conservation staff of the Department of Manuscripts in the British Library. The late Victor Carter and Tony Parker both took a vivid interest in the research on the Malory Manuscript and were always ready to offer practical assistance and suggestions for new methods of investigation. In the later stages, the Library's Chief Photographer, Graham Marsh, and his staff provided active help in bringing the research to completion. I feel also particularly grateful to them for their contribution to the illustration of the present book, not least to Graham Marsh for climbing pews in order to photograph the stained-glass window in St Margaret's, Westminster, on the one hot afternoon of the year 1981.

I received valuable comments on the text while it was in preparation from my husband and from my colleagues Dr Margaret Nickson, Nicolas Barker, Dr Paul Needham and Ian Willison, who all read early drafts or sections of the text, and whose observations caused me to make changes. Of course they cannot be held responsible for any errors or opinions. I am much obliged to Christopher Walker and Helen Smith for the attention they gave to editorial questions. It was a delight to see the book take shape in the hands of Sebastian Carter. Finally I have felt grateful throughout for the encouragement and help offered by Hugh Cobbe, Jane Carr and John Mitchell.

London, June 1982   LOTTE HELLINGA

List of Illustrations

Colour Plates

Figures

22. Two forms of I in Type 2 in verse.

23. Two forms of I in Type 2 used in prose.

24. Two forms of *a*, distinct use in the *Cordiale* printed in Bruges.

25. *Horae ad usum Sarum*. Double *a* is used at the beginning of words.

26. The name *arcite* is set with double *a* in the *Canterbury Tales*.

27. Double *a* used for the titles of books in the *Canterbury Tales*.

28. Shortage of round *a*'s in *The History of Jason*.

29. The list of collective nouns in the Cambridge copy of *The Horse, the Sheep and the Goose*.

30. The list of collective nouns in the copy of *The Horse, the Sheep and the Goose* in the Pierpont Morgan Library.

31. A combination of light and heavy type designed by Johannes Veldener, used in Bruges, *c*.1477.

32. Caxton's Type 3 as used by Johannes Veldener in a Herbal.

33. Caxton's Type 2 and Type 3 used in deliberate contrast in his *Boethius*, 1478.

34. H of Type 3 used in Type 2 to accentuate Jason's exclamations.

35. Caxton's Type 3 used in Antwerp by Mathias van der Goes, *c*.1488.

36. Caxton's Type 3 used in Louvain by Rudolphus Loeffs de Driel.

37. Type 3 used in London by John Lettou and William de Machlinia, *c*. 1482.

38. Caxton's Type 3 used at St. Albans by the Schoolmaster Printer, 1486.

39. Caxton's Type 3 used by Wynkyn de Worde in 1495.

40. Detail of Caxton's Indulgence of 1476, the name (I)Ohannes printed in Type 3.

41. The colophon in the Lambeth manuscript of *The Dictes and Sayengs of the Philosophers*.

42. The beginning of Caxton's epilogue to the *Dictes* with the date 1477.

43. Signature of Earl Rivers with his motto.

44. Caxton's own verse at the end of Earl Rivers' translation of the *Moral Proverbs* of Christine de Pisan.

45. Caxton's colophon to Earl Rivers' translation of the *Cordiale*, 1479.

46. A calendar according to Sarum usage, printed by Wynkyn de Worde, *c*.1494.

47. Offsets of capitals I and F of Caxton types in the Malory manuscript, taken from the screen of the Video Spectral Comparator.

48. Reversed image of the offset of capital I of Type 2, taken from the Visualtek screen.

49. The end of page g 1 verso and the beginning of page g 2 recto in Caxton's edition of Thomas Malory, *Morte Darthur*.

50. The same passage in the Malory manuscript.

51. The setting of the first quire of *The History of Jason*.

52. The beginning of the text of *The History of Jason* in Caxton's translation.

William Caxton

William Caxton is the only English printer to be numbered among the great men of the nation's collective memory. His reputation rests on the hundred books he published between 1473 and 1492, on some twenty works he translated into English, and on the fact that he was the first Englishman to become actively involved in the then new art of printing. After a rather tentative beginning in Cologne and Bruges, he introduced printing into England, an experiment which he turned into a flourishing enterprise. But leaving aside his priority in technical and commercial fields, Caxton still appeals to us because he addressed his readers personally, and with a directness that remains vivid to the present day. Caxton included in many of his publications an explanation of his reasons for giving the text he printed a wider readership, and of the circumstances under which he had prepared it. He would indicate the readers for whom the book was intended, and discuss who had advised him to publish it, to whom it was dedicated, and would ponder his own role in the venture. Thus, dedicating his translation of a romance to Lady Margaret Beaufort, the Queen Mother, he addressed her in this way: '. . . *Bysechynge my sayd ladyes bountyuous grace to receyve this lityll boke in gree of me, her humble servaunt, and to pardoune me of the rude and comyn Englyshe, where as shall be found faulte; for I confesse me not lerned ne knowynge the arte of rethoryk ne of suche gaye termes as now be sayd in these dayes and used. Bat I hope that it shall be understonden of the redars and herers – and that shall suffyse.*' Caxton wrote this after about twenty years' experience as author and translator. He had shown an acute sense of language ever since he had begun his first translation from the French, *The Recuyell of the Historyes of Troye*, in 1468. Translating the first pages he was '*renning forth*', as he put it, '*as blynde Bayard*', and became conscious of his '*symplenes and unperfightnes in bothe langages*'. Nevertheless, despite experiencing a fit of despair he persisted, encouraged by Margaret of York, Duchess of Burgundy, who ordered him to continue his translation, but only after some demurring on his part, and after she had corrected '*a defaute in myn Englissh*'. Towards the end of his career, in his translation of Virgil, he was capable of a sharper formulation of the questions that still plagued him. '*Certaynly it is harde to playse every man bycause of dyversite and chaunge of langage. For in these dayes every man that is in ony reputacyon in his countre wyll utter his commynycacyon and maters in suche maners and termes that fewe men shall understonde theym. And som honest and grete clerkes have ben wyth me and desired me to wryte the moste curyous termes that I coude fynde. And thus bytwene*

13

playn rude and curyous I stande abasshed. . . . Therfor in a meane bytwene bothe I have reduced and translated this sayd booke in to our englysshe not over rude ne curyous, but in suche termes as shall be understanden by goddys grace, accordynge to my copye. . .' These words are certainly more than a modest disclaimer inspired by convention. He thereby showed himself aware of local diversity of language, and also of variety of language as an indicator of social position. A lifetime spent abroad, in a French and Dutch-speaking world (he knew both languages well), may have sharpened Caxton's sensitive ear to the social nuances of his mother tongue.

He never ceased to marvel that it was he *'symple person William Caxton'*, to whom the responsibility had fallen of publishing these books in print. He continually queried his own adequacy to the task: was this the correct form, the correct language, was the text complete, did he give good value, would it please? His self-doubt is captivating.

Perhaps there were ample grounds for self-doubt. Caxton's education had not equipped him for dealing with literary works, and in public life he had climbed quite high on the social scale. This is one reason why we know very little of his early life. The year and place of his birth are unknown. According to his own words he was born in Kent, and we may reasonably assume that this was around the year 1422. His family relationships are not directly documented, and have given rise to lengthy arguments and speculations. The earliest document to give a firm indication of his activities is the entry in the Warden's Account of the Mercers' Company, which records Caxton's enrolment in the year 1437/8 as an apprentice to the London wool merchant Robert Large. When still a young man, perhaps even when still an apprentice, Caxton moved to Bruges, which was then one of the most important centres of trade in Europe, and which harboured the headquarters of the Guild of the Merchant Adventurers, the main company of the English wool traders. Caxton was to pass thirty years in the western Low Countries – according to his own words in Flanders, Brabant, Holland and Zeeland, but mainly in the great cities of Flanders, Bruges and Ghent.

In those years he gradually rose to a position of eminence among his fellow merchants. We see him appearing in documents as arbitrator in local disputes where English mercantile interests were concerned, and as a negotiator on behalf of others. His reputation evidently increased, and by 1462 he had become Governor of the settlement of English merchants in Bruges, known as the English Nation. His actions in this capacity are only patchily documented, where records of representation or arbitration happen to have survived. But it is evident that this was a position of great responsibility, and in many ways foreshadowed the lesser roles which diplomats were to play in later times. Caxton's position of eminence

14

within his own class brought him in touch with the highest circles of both countries. He could call himself the devoted servant of the King of England, of the King's sister Margaret, Duchess of Burgundy, and of other members of the royal entourage. We have a portrait of Caxton (see Fig. 6) as the trusted courtier and mainstay of the English settlement of merchants overseas. It is a contemporary copper engraving (in itself an unusual and novel medium at that time for pictorial representation), and is probably an accurate likeness, since the other known person, the Duchess Margaret, can confidently be identified by her initials and her motto 'Bien en aviegne', and resembles her known portraits. We see how Caxton presented to her his first work of translation, *The Recuyell of the Historyes of Troye*. It was a turning point in his life.

This had been preceded, as so often happens, by a crisis. Its origins remain largely obscure, but must probably be sought in the vicissitudes of the relations between the courts of England and Burgundy. Whatever the cause, Caxton suddenly left Flanders in the summer of 1471 and spent eighteen months in exile in Cologne. Here, in a city with an important university and an intellectual influence that made itself felt in the entire north-west of Europe, a printing house had been established in 1465, followed within a few years by others. They printed first for the university and for the many religious houses in the city, but soon for a rapidly expanding market. Books printed in Cologne followed the trade routes and were shipped far and wide. By that time Caxton the merchant must also have been an enthusiastic reader and lover of books. The opportunities offered by the new technique were not lost on him. In Cologne he learned how to print, and sponsored the production of a large book, an encyclopaedic work, *De proprietatibus rerum*, by Bartholomaeus Anglicus. On his return to Flanders, after Christmas 1472, he wasted no time in establishing a press there making use of connexions he had made in Cologne, and published his first literary work, in English. Only a few years later, after publication in Flanders of some seven books in English and French, he decided to move his publishing business to England, where, after an absence of thirty years, he set up a press in the precincts of Westminster Abbey.

It is only from this point that Caxton's career is fully documented, almost exclusively through the books he printed. There are the familiar mile-stones, the *Canterbury Tales*, Thomas Malory's *Le Morte Darthur*, books which have been in demand ever since Caxton printed them. There are also many books that are now forgotten but were fashionable at the time. They include Caxton's own translations. Many of them were new to the English public since Caxton introduced works he had come to know on the continent. There can be no doubt that there were further books that are now lost. As Caxton's publications survive today they form an impressive and attractive sequence, a monument to one man's delight in sharing with others his respect for texts (to which he gave a new form) and his pleasure in reading them.

Caxton died on the day he completed yet another long translation, that of the *Vitas Patrum*, or *Lyves of holy faders lyvynge in deserte*. The date of his death is not known, but it probably took place early in 1492. He was buried in St. Margaret's, Westminster.

The date of almost every material fact of Caxton's life eludes us. In the present book I intend to concentrate only on one event, Caxton's introduction of printing into England. There is little documentary evidence to rely on. We have to examine closely the internal evidence of the books he produced in the first phase of his activity as a printer. Their dating will concern us, but close examination reveals more to us than the circumstances of their production alone. In the course of investigating these books we shall also have to consider how the evidence they present has been interpreted before, and past assess-ments of Caxton's position as England's arch-typographer. We shall see that these have changed considerably over the centuries. As Caxton himself wrote: '. . .*We englysshe men ben borne under the domynacyon of the mone, whiche is never stedfaste, but ever waverynge, wexynge one season and waneth and dyscreaseth another season. . .*' His own fate and that of his bibliographers could not have been better expressed.

Investigating early books

The appeal of early printed books may lie in their beauty, their rarity or their curiosity. They can be sources for textual studies, and some early printed books like Caxton's *Canterbury Tales* may still be read for pleasure. But whatever their significance in these respects, and no matter what the contents, they are also material objects, the products of an intricate mechanical process. Therefore, if we wish to write their history, we have to investigate their physical make-up, just as we do for other objects made in the past. Whether we are concerned with incunabula (that is books printed before 1501) or with books of a later period, research into the history of books requires an understanding of book-production. First, a book has to be described in detail, and this may involve the examination of minutiae the printers of the book thought to be unimportant, or perhaps hoped would go unnoticed. A researcher may chase a peculiar form of a printing type, peer at watermarks or scrutinize stains and smudges. Trifling mishaps in the printing house may now get a degree of attention that seems out of proportion to the events that once caused them or to the effect of the blemishes on the final product. Yet sometimes, with luck, these scraps of information may throw light on the production process and when pieced together, may even add substantially to the history of printing.

The investigation of early printed books uses magnifying glasses, special lamps, and even more intriguing instruments; we are on the trail of the ancient equivalents of match-ends and fingerprints, and the process is often compared to detective work. 'It reads like a thriller', the readers of reports of such investigations may say; and yet the compliment is received with mixed feelings. The resemblance cannot be denied, but the task of relating the observations to actual historical circumstances is usually much more demanding than the sleuthing itself. For this reason archaeology offers a more accurate comparison. 'Archaeology of the book' is a term that is beginning to find acceptance for the material investigation of books.

Books, however, have an eloquence all their own. Unlike other artefacts, and unlike (to a certain extent) pictorial art, they are capable of delivering statements on their own behalf as witnesses to the past. By definition books contain texts, and part of their contents may be a short text concerned with the making of the book itself. Books can tell us in their own words, in an imprint or colophon, who made them, where they were printed, when and by whom, and sometimes even tell us at greater length under what circumstances, for whom and why. We have to pay close attention to what they say about themselves, to take their statements very seriously indeed; but we must not fall into the trap of taking their words at face value. Our use of language is no longer the same as that of incunables; and what was true in the fifteenth century may not have the same truth value in the present. We may have to call in other witnesses in order to assess the value of the words with which we are presented and we may have to weigh it against material evidence. Also, books can unintentionally reveal a great deal about how they were made through the complete text which they contain. We can study the text as it was issued by the printer, compare it with other versions in print or in manuscript, and in rare moments we may even be lucky enough to catch the actual transition from a manuscript into print. These studies bring us closer to the minds of those actively engaged in making a book with the purpose of transmitting a text in this particular medium. It is one way of observing books as witnesses of the past.

Books cannot always be assumed to be perfect witnesses intent on speaking the truth. On the contrary, books can lie, and go on misleading us for centuries. In such cases, as in the courtroom, the book's honesty is assumed until proved otherwise. The burden of proof lies with us, in the present. Whether an untruth is a mistake or a deliberate lie, it has to be exposed on the basis of facts provided by the investigator. Experts may be called in to explain how and why it all happened, as far as possible. However, in the end it is not the books on whom judgement will be passed, but the methods and conclusions of their successive investigators.

Take for example the introduction of printing into England. A simple case. When did the deed take place? It seems straightforward: there is a book that states that it was printed in Oxford in 1468. It survives in thirteen copies and the same colophon is printed in each of them: 'Impressa Oxonie Et finita Anno domini. M.cccc. lxviij.xvij. die decembris' (see Fig. 1). The next book printed in England to bear an unambiguous date says that it was completed by William Caxton in Westminster on 18 November 1477 (see Colour plate 1). On the face of it Oxford therefore clearly preceded Westminster. In fact we now know that neither claimant, intentionally or not, spoke the truth. But why? It is only now, after more than three centuries of discussion, that we begin to understand why and how it came about that they were both untruthful. Also, it is only now that we can state with confidence that we do not know exactly when the introduction of printing into England took place.

In this book I propose to concentrate on the few years when printing was first established in England. The arrival of the printing press heralded a revolutionary development in intellectual life and in society wherever it took place. This has of course long been recognized, and in consequence the invention of printing and its

18

qui refurgunt in vitam eternam·literati
vero a confufione et obprobrio eterno ·
per criftum dominum noftrum per quem
é deo patri ommipotéti cũ fpiritu fancto
gloria et imperium in fecula feculorum
amen ·

Explicit expoficio fancti Jeronimi in
fimbolo apoftolorum ad papam laurē
cium Impreſſa Oxonie Et finita An
no domini · M · cccc · lxviij · xvij·die
decembris ·

1. The earliest date associated with printing in England. Colophon showing the date
'1468' in the first book printed in Oxford. British Library, 167.b.26, leaf e 9 verso.

emplum et confequentia naturalis
rationis affignet. Si inquam hec fecũ
dum traditionis fupra expofite re
gulam confequamur aduertimus
depreemur ut nobis et omnibus
qui hoc audiunt concedat dominus
fide quam fufcepimus cuftodia curfu
confumato expectare uiftine repofi-
tam coronam et inueniri inter eos
qui refurgunt in uiiam eternam
liberari uero a confufione et obpro
brio eterno· per xpium dominum no
ftrum per quem eft deo patri omni
potenti cum fpu fancto gloria et im
perium in fecula feculorum amen

finis laus deo

2. Manuscript used as printer's copy for the first book printed in Oxford, end of text.
Three dots mark the beginning of the last page in the Oxford book.   British Library,
MS Sloane 1579, leaf 50 verso.

spread throughout Europe has attracted a vast amount of research and literature since the late sixteenth century. Yet the precise chronology and hence the precise circumstances of the beginning of printing presses are in many instances obscure, and printing in England is no exception. In the last three centuries its history has been written many times with ever varying shifts in emphasis. As in every historical subject, each age has its own interpretation. In the last few years the development of bibliographical studies has imposed higher standards of precision on methods of investigation and this has brought to light new information. It is therefore time to shake the kaleidoscope once again and to take a fresh look at the pattern into which the facts, some old, some new, will fall this time. In the first place this will lead to a new chronological arrangement. In itself this will change our view of the intentions with which England's first printer started on his publishing venture. But in reviewing the facts we shall also learn more about his relations to his patrons, about his intended public and about the way his printing house worked.

In order to take a fresh look there has to be a dual approach. Despite a desire to concentrate entirely on investigating the documents that have come down to us, we must also query the reasons for our accepted way of thinking. We must pay attention to the facts which were available to our predecessors and how they arranged them, in order to understand their interpretation and to assess their and our own judgements and prejudices. It is a procedure as demanding as uncovering new facts, but it never fails to have its rewards. To understand *why*, you have to dig. In this case we must reach back to the time when the introduction of printing into England first aroused more interest than mere chronicling. We therefore have to return to the Oxford book.

The Oxford legend

RICHARD ATKYNS

Oxford's claim to be the first city in England to see a printing house at work might have been given much more serious consideration if it had come from a reputable source. It might even have eclipsed the fame Caxton began to enjoy in the eighteenth century. As it was the opposite happened and Caxton's reputation flourished as the Oxford story was discredited.

Until well into the seventeenth century early printing in England attracted scant attention and had only been mentioned in passing by the main chroniclers and historiographers. Early printing in general had been taken largely for granted, with the exception of the beginning of the dispute between the cities of Mainz and Haarlem, rival contenders for the honour of having harboured the inventor of printing, respectively Johannes Gutenberg and Laurens Janszoon Coster. The origins of this dispute lie in early nationalistic sentiments and also in sheer political manoeuvring in claiming privileges from authority. Politics were an important element in the claims made for Haarlem in 1588 in the then very young Dutch Republic.

The Oxford claim offers a curious parallel to the Dutch case. In 1664, four years after the Restoration, Richard Atkyns (1615–1677), an impoverished gentleman, wrote a little book, *The Original and Growth of Printing*, in order to point out to King Charles II that the monopoly of printing did not belong to the Stationers' Company in London, who were unfit, in his opinion, to put it to proper use. 'That *printing*', he wrote 'belongs to Your Majesty, in Your publique and private Capacity as Supream Magistrate, and as Proprietor, I do with all boldness affirm; and that it is a considerable *branch* of the *Regal Power*', for '. . . *Where the Word of a King is there is Power*'. In support of this topical thesis Atkyns produced two pieces of evidence. One was a document which he claimed to have seen in the archives of the Archbishop of Canterbury in Lambeth Palace; the other one was a book, the *Expositio in symbolum apostolorum*, which had hitherto remained unnoticed. The book was completed in Oxford, according to its colophon, on 17 December 1468.

The Lambeth document purported to bring a sinister plot to light. Thomas Bourchier, Archbishop of Canterbury, and King Henry VI had conspired, not long after 1460, to steal the secrets of the newly invented art of printing from the continent and to bring them to England. The document and the book were cleverly brought together by Richard Atkyns to fabricate a story which contains most of the names hitherto connected with the invention of printing. It relates how a certain Corcellis, servant of the inventor, Johannes Gutenberg at Haarlem (an ingenuous conflation of the two pretenders), aided and abetted by a Mr Caxton, was bribed to leave his master and to flee to England, and was held in seclusion in Oxford until he had taught the craft to some Englishmen. This whole secret operation was financed by the king of England. Therefore, concluded Atkyns, it is crystal clear that the king's successors, and no one else, had direct authority by hereditary right over the printing presses of the realm. Atkyns' claim does not seem to have made any noticeable impact, and failed to benefit his own pocket, as he had hoped. He died ten years later in poverty. But the legend lingered on.

CONYERS MIDDLETON

It took a long time, however, before a genuine interest in the early printing history of England had developed sufficiently for someone to judge a refutation necessary. When it came at last, it distinguished fact from fabrication, weighed the evidence and came up with a carefully considered conclusion. It was Conyers Middleton (1683–1750), a great controversialist and librarian of the Public University Library in Cambridge, who thus in 1735 showed those qualities which were to adorn a long tradition of British bibliographical scholarship. Middleton dismissed as 'fabulous' the Lambeth document, which apparently nobody since Atkyns had been able to discover, but had to conclude: 'We have now cleared our hands of the Record, but the Book stands firm, as a Monument of the Exercise of Printing in Oxford.' Indeed it stands firm to this day, as we have seen in the surviving thirteen copies, all with the same colophon. Conyers Middleton found it difficult to disprove the veracity of the Oxford book. He attempted to do this by using the argument of Caxton's silence on the subject. In view of Caxton's usual expansiveness on anything that took his interest, this does indeed weaken the strength of the Oxford claim. However, there is better evidence, but this was not yet available in Middleton's time.

THE DATING OF THE FIRST OXFORD BOOK

The Oxford *Expositio*, and two other books also printed in Oxford which are obviously closely related to it and which both bear the date 1479, are printed in a type that was also used in Cologne and in

Deventer. For a number of reasons it is certain that the type was first used in Cologne (and manufactured there) and taken over by several printers who worked elsewhere, and not made in Oxford and used elsewhere later. It was used in Cologne by the printer Gerhard ten Raem, who printed dated editions in this type in the years 1477 and 1478. It is only since the beginning of this century that we have been able to set out these facts. In 1903 a bibliography of Cologne printing was published by Ernst Voulliéme, and it is due to his work that we can be reasonably confident that we know which types were used by Cologne printers, and when. A printing type cannot be used before its manufacture – a simple argument much used in printing history, although even it is not unassailable, as we shall see with Caxton. For the first Oxford book the argument was not sufficient entirely to convince Falconer Madan, the author of the bibliography of Oxford printing (whose first volume was published in 1895), who still expressed some reservations when he completed his work in 1931: 'The cumulative evidence . . . does not yet amount to positive proof'. In spite of this Oxford celebrated its quincentenary of printing in the year 1978 with no one dissenting.

But there still remains the question of the date 1468 in the colophon of the *Expositio*. As a mistake it is curious, but there is no circumstance that indicates a deliberate act of deception. Nothing is more difficult to explain than a simple mistake, especially when it means, as it does here, that a date is no less than ten years wrong. The usual explanation, ever since Middleton, is that an x in the roman figure was left out, or dropped out in the dating 'Impressa Oxonie Et finita Anno domini M.cccc.lxviij.xvij. die decembris.' This kind of typographical mishap is not impossible; several instances can be quoted from the fifteenth century. As a sole explanation it is nevertheless not quite satisfactory. However, in the quincentenary year a fact came to light (in a roundabout way) that provided evidence that may indicate more than a mere coincidence. Dr A. C. de la Mare discovered among the Sloane collection in the British Library the manuscript that had served as printer's copy for the Oxford *Expositio*. It was written in Florence for a scholarly public in the early 1440s, and brought to England by the bookloving bishop James Goldwell (d. 1499). Extensive textual comparison showed that the compositor of the Oxford book, striving after textual correctness where the Goldwell manuscript was unsatisfactory to him, occasionally consulted an edition of the same text, contained in a large publication of related texts printed in Rome in 1468, and took over some of the readings of the printed book in preference to the manuscript source. When he arrived at the end of setting his own small book and wished to formulate a colophon he found none in the manuscript (see Fig. 2). The compositor may then again have looked to the book printed in Rome for an example. The words

23

dating it at the end ' . . . anno christi M.CCCC.LXVIII. indictione prima. die vero.xiii.mensis decembris' (See Fig. 3) may have prompted his hand to set 'M.cccc.lxviij', rather than a fit of entirely spontaneous absentmindedness.

racula gloriosa: explicandi ea nullatenus compos essem. Ceci sedecim illas reliquias tangentes: facte usum pristinum receperunt. Tres precipue demoniaci cathenis uincti: in illam ecclesiam plurimorum hominum manibus deportati: sunt protinus liberati. Mulieris cuiusdam uidue paupercule puerulus: eius unicus filius: in ecclesia fuit pre gentium multitudine suffocatus: quem mater inueniens: dolens & lugens: mox in ulnis pueruli cadauer ad foueam in qua sepultum fuerat corpus Hieronymi gloriosi deferret: eum in foueam proiecit. hec dicens uerba. Sancte Hieronyme gloriose: hinc non recedam: donec restituas mihi unicum meum filium quem amisi. Mirabilis certe deus in sanctis suis: faciens prodigia insueta. statim ut terram extincti pueruli corpus: tetigit: eidem anima est coniuncta. Quidam uir corpus cuisdam sui filii de sepultura: in qua p triduum steterat extractum: mox ad foueam illam detulit: et illud in foueam sic iecit: q iuuenis fuit ilico uite pristine restitutus. Innumerabilia pene forent miracula: que pacta sunt a mane usqʒ ad uesperas: quo qdem tempore gloriosi Hieronymi cadauer de fouea dissepultum in altari extiti: collocatum. Sed tamen ad huiusmodi miracula ulterius non procedam. Vnum quod nocte sequenti accidit: non silebo.

IN hora siqdem uespertina corpus illud sacratissimum in monumeto qd preparauimus posuimus: sed mane monum:ʒtum uacuum est inuentum. et corpus sanctissimum fouee pristine inuenimus restitutum. Quod dum ego plurimum admirarer: nocte sequenti mihi dormienti beatus Hieronymus apparens in uisione: plurima mihi grandia patefecit. Sed inter cetera talia mihi uerba dixit. Noueris Cyrille: qp corpus meum de fouea in qua iacet: nullatenus extrahetur. quousqʒ ciuitas hierusalem ab infidelibus capietur. Quo qdem tempore roma delatum: ibidem multo tempore regescet. Ad hec expgefactus: que uideram cū ctis episcopis & aliis uiris catholicis enarraui. Quid et qñ hec eueniet: aliter non agnosco. Si quid utile aut bonum in hac epistola dixi: non meis sed glorio/ sissimi Hieronymi meritis imputetur. Si quid uero superfluum inutile & non bonum: solum mee insipientie et negligentie causa hoc accidisse: ab omnibus iudicetur. Mei Augustine carissime in tuis orationibus memor esto.

Eusebii Hieronymi doctoris eximii secudum epistolarum explicit uolumen. anno christi. M. CCCC. LXVIII. Indictione prima. die uero. xiii. mensis decembris. Pontifice maximo Paulo regnante secudo. anno eius quinto.

Rome in domo magnifici uiri Petri de Maximo.

3. Colophon of Hieronymus, *Epistolae* printed in Rome in 1468, consulted by the compositor in the course of setting the first Oxford book. British Library, C.13.e.2, leaf [HH] 11 verso.

Caxton studies in the eighteenth century

In spite of the fact that there was the occasional adherent of Oxford's claim, Caxton's reputation in the eighteenth century as England's first printer, and the first printer in the English language, went from strength to strength.

Middleton's *Dissertation* of 1735 was very rapidly followed by a more extensive work, *The Life of Mayster Wyllyam Caxton* by the Rev. John Lewis (1675–1747) which appeared only two years later, in 1737. Unlike Middleton's work Lewis's book was a full-scale biographical study, and as there was at the time very little known about Caxton apart from what can be learned from his books, what Lewis presented was more in the nature of a bibliography. Lewis listed the Caxton editions that were known to him, and reconstructed from them an outline of Caxton's life. It was in the preceding decade that, for the first time, a large number of Caxton's books had been brought together in the very important library of the Earls of Oxford, called the Harleian Library. The Caxtons were assembled by Edward, the second Earl, (1689–1741) in a later phase of the collection, and were partly acquired as a result of the arrival on the market of earlier, smaller collections. The Harleian books were generously made accessible to scholars, and the library has had therefore a very significant impact on the development of the knowledge of the history of printing and bibliographical scholarship in general. One of its librarians, Randall Minshull, planned at one stage to publish a separate bibliography of Caxton editions, but in the end contented himself with putting the material he had assembled at the disposal of Caxton's next bibliographer, Joseph Ames. The dispersal, after 1742, of the printed books in the Harleian collection gave great impetus to the formation of other collections. Today Harleian copies are treasured items found in many of the great collections of early printed books.

BOOK COLLECTING AND BIBLIOGRAPHICAL STUDIES

The Harleian Library, then, had a decisive influence on early bibliographical work on Caxton. From this date book collecting directly influenced scholarship, and *vice versa*. It established a tradition that was happily to continue for a long time. Book collecting brought new information to light, and this information was incorporated in growing bibliographical compilations on early

25

printing. For English printing a history which amounts to an extensive bibliography was several times published in updated versions. Meanwhile copies of these works, now precious, were annotated by the diligent collectors-cum-bibliographers (see Fig. 4).

Caxton's books were singled out for special attention. Most of the

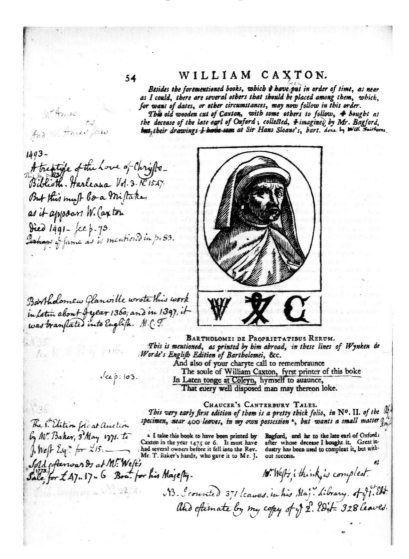

4. A copy of Joseph Ames, *Typographical Antiquities*, 1749, annotated by the author and by William Herbert. This page documents the history of the King's Library copy of the *Canterbury Tales*.   British Library, C.60.0.5, p.54.

5. Binding of the King's Library copy of the *Canterbury Tales*, bound for an unknown collector around the middle of the eighteenth century. The arms of King George III were added later.   British Library, 167.c.26.

copies now extant received, in the eighteenth century, the form in which they survive today. Original volumes combining more than one publication were split. Their early plain leather bindings on thick wooden boards were discarded in favour of the eighteenth-century livery of coloured leather adorned with gold (see Fig. 5). Traces of the past like early notes of ownership were washed away, or when they occurred on grubby but dispensable blank leaves, simply ripped out. Worst of all, collectors exchanged damaged leaves for good ones from incomplete copies, leaving hybrids to confuse the bibliographer of the twentieth century. Apparently the books were expected to look in some ways 'as new'.

Yet, even if we feel a tinge of regret for the treatment of books in this period, the impetus of collecting on bibliography was extraordinary. The impression has been created that this pursuit was confined to the nobility. However, most collectors after the dispersal of the Harleian Library until the nineteenth century belonged to various strata of society within the mercantile class. Usually they won general respect for their knowledge; only occasionally was a collector, such as John Ratcliffe, the possessor of one of the finest collections of early English printing, sneered at for his lack of culture. Nobody, however, felt above buying his books, when they came up for auction.

JOSEPH AMES AND HIS FOLLOWERS

Many of Caxton's early bibliographers were self-taught men. After John Lewis came Joseph Ames (1689–1759), who must be considered as the founding-father of British bibliography. As a young man he was encouraged by Caxton's first biographer and, as we have seen, by Randall Minshull to attempt a more ambitious work. In 1749 he completed the first edition of *Typographical Antiquities*, which encompassed all English printing to the year 1600. Ames in his turn encouraged his younger friend William Herbert (1718–1795), who like Ames, owned a major collection of English printing. Herbert published between 1785 and 1790 a revised edition of Ames' book which included much material that had come to light in the intermediate 40 years of great activity in book-collecting. Finally the librarian of the collection of Earl Spencer, the Rev. Thomas Frognall Dibdin (1776–1847) brought this phase in bibliographical work on Caxton (and other early printers in England) to an end in 1810 with the publication of the last version of Ames' *Antiquities*, further enlarged by an irrepressible and sometimes gullible capacity for gossip and anecdotes.

Ames' work was in this way continued by Herbert and Dibdin and it brought into clear focus the picture of Caxton as the enterprising merchant who introduced printing into England. The products of his press were listed and described with increasing accuracy. Ames provided quotations from the lengthy texts which Caxton had written to accompany many of his publications. These are a feature of Caxton's work that is unusual in fifteenth-century printing and has seldom been parallelled in later times. But in spite of what may appear to be a torrent of information, Caxton leaves the reader surprisingly often in the dark as to place and date of publication. This is particularly true of the sizeable group of books held to be his earliest.

The earliest date ever mentioned by Caxton himself is found in *The Recuyell of the Historyes of Troye*. (See Colour plate 11) The prologues and epilogues he wrote to accompany this book have become famous pieces of prose and have been quoted frequently. Amid much charming circumlocution (Caxton seldom used one word if he could use two or more, as a matter of elegant deportment), a number of facts emerge which are of central importance for an understanding of Caxton's life:

He was born in the Weald of Kent.

He had spent at the time of writing thirty years of his life in the western part of the Low Countries, that is in Brabant, Flanders, Holland and Zeeland.

He had never been to France.

The text he translated from French into English was a collection of legends about the city of Troy compiled by the priest Raoul le Fèvre, who had completed this work in 1464 and dedicated it to Philip the Good, Duke of Burgundy.

Caxton had started the translation in a period of leisure, but had laid it aside, feeling inadequate to the task since his English had grown rusty.

He had started the work in Bruges, on 1 March 1468, and had laid it aside for two years.

He had been summoned about two years later by Margaret of York, Duchess of Burgundy and sister of King Edward IV to discuss various matters. Margaret of York had married Charles the Bold, Duke of Burgundy, on 3 July 1468; everyone knew that, because it was the most glittering marriage of its day (and its memory lives on even today in Bruges).

When Caxton's work as translator was mentioned in his discussion with the young duchess, she demanded that it be shown to her, corrected at once an error in Caxton's English, but nevertheless commissioned him to complete his translation.

He could not disobey this command as he was in her service.

He subsequently worked on his translation in Ghent and in Cologne. It is not clear whether part of this second phase was carried out in Bruges.

He completed the work in Cologne on 19 September 1471.

6. The dedication of *The Recuyell of the Historyes of Troye* by Caxton to Margaret of York, Duchess of Burgundy. Contemporary engraving preserved in one copy. San Marino, Henry E. Huntington Library.

In Cologne he had too much time on his hands. He therefore learned the art of printing, at great expense, and the result is the book as the reader has it before him.

The book as translated by Caxton was dedicated to Margaret of York, was graciously accepted by her and he was nobly rewarded by her.

Two facts are conspicuously absent here: the place of printing of the *Recuyell* and the date.

CAXTON'S DATING OF THE *RECUYELL* AS INTERPRETED IN THE EIGHTEENTH CENTURY

These two questions have exercised the ingenuity of all Caxton's bibliographers. Middleton surmised that the *Recuyell* was printed in Cologne, Lewis was more cautious and thought of Bruges as a possibility; Ames, however, decided that it was printed in Cologne, in 1471, shortly after the translation was completed. He gave it pride of place as the first book known to have been printed in English. In this position of honour it was left by all subsequent bibliographers who, however, thought that Caxton preceded it by an edition of the same text in French and by a little book in Latin. Everyone agreed that wherever these books were printed (and Cologne was really the only place that came up in the discussion), it was not in England.

DATE AND PLACE OF PRINTING OF *THE GAME OF CHESS*

There is considerable ambiguity about the next date mentioned by Caxton himself. It is the year 1474 with which Caxton ended his translation of Jacobus de Cessolis, *The Game of Chess*, a work of moral allegory, very popular on the continent but almost unknown in England at that time. He dedicated it to another royal patron, the Duke of Clarence, brother of the King. He ended the printed book with the words: 'Fynysshid the last day of marche the yer of our lord god .a. thousand foure honderd and .lxxiiii.' (see Fig. 7). Caxton does not make it clear whether this date refers to the translation or to the printing of the book; over the last hundred years it has been commonly argued that, according to the French year style (often used in Flanders), whereby the year began at Easter, the date should be interpreted as 1475. When Caxton reprinted *The Game of Chess*

31

In conquerynge his rightfull enheritaunce / that verray
peas and charite may endure in bothe his royames / and
that marchandise may haue his cours in suche wise that
euery man eschewe synne / and encrece in vertuous occu-
pacions / Prayinge your good grace to resseyue this lityll
and symple book made vnder the hope and shadowe of
your noble protection by hym that is your most humble
seruant / in gree and thanke And I shall praye almighty
god for your longe lyf a welfare / whiche he preserue
And sende yow thaccomplisshement of your hye noble.
Joyous and vertuous desire Amen :/: Fynysshid the
last day of marche the yer of our lord god.a.thousand
foure honderd and lxxiiii .·:·:·.

7. Jacobus de Cessolis, *The Game of Chess*, translated by Caxton. Colophon, with
disputed date. British Library, C.10.b.23, leaf [i] 9 recto.

some years later in Westminster he wrote in a prologue that he had
seen the book when he was resident in Bruges and had undertaken
the translation there. The eighteenth-century bibliographers
accepted without question the date 1474 as applying to the
completion of printing, but they differed in their opinion as to the
place of printing, and therefore in the importance they attached to
the book. Ames held that the book was the first to be printed in
England; his main argument in support of this contention was the
coincidence he saw between the dating of the book and the curious
shapes in the centre of Caxton's device, which he read as 7 and λ
(an early form for the arabic numeral 4), which could be combined
to the figure 74. Ames thought that Caxton commemorated in his
device (which he did not use until 1487) the year when he
introduced printing into England (see Fig. 8). Ames' subsequent
editors, Herbert and Dibdin, did not commit themselves on this
point.

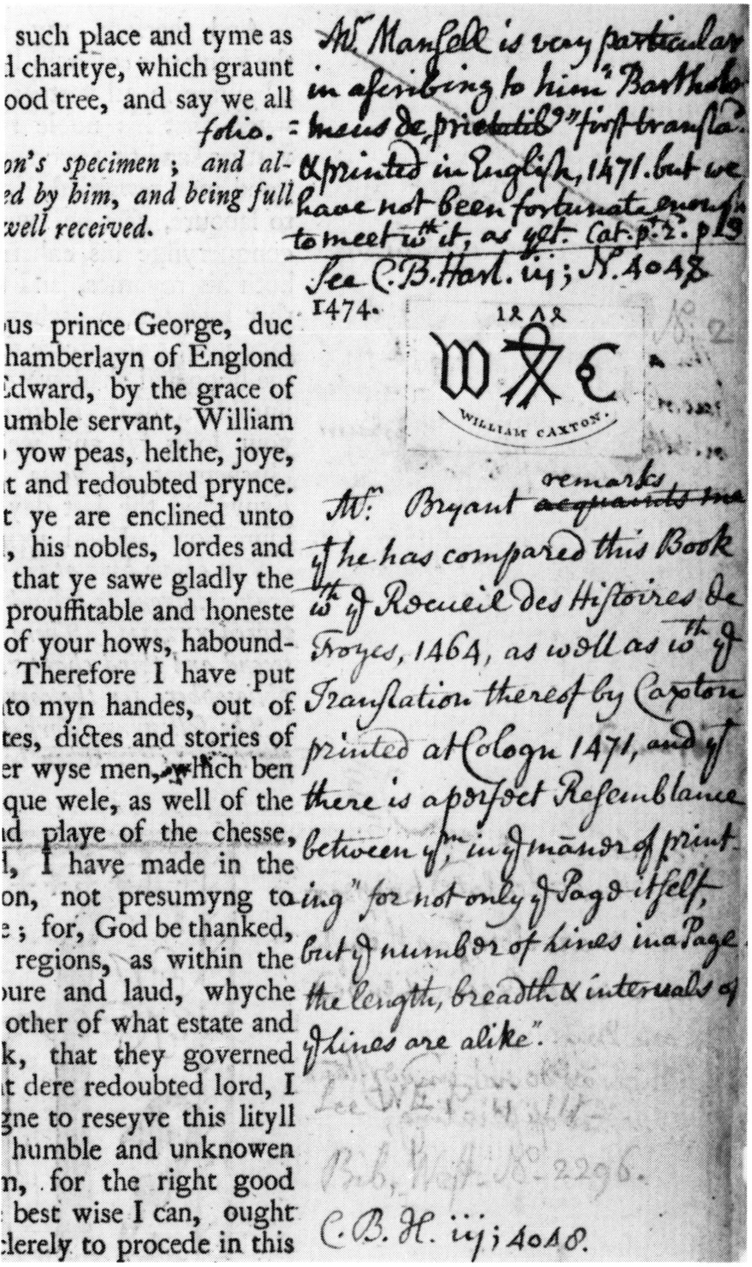
such place and tyme as
d charitye, which graunt
ood tree, and say we all
folio.
on's specimen ; and al-
ed by him, and being full
well received.

ous prince George, duc
hamberlayn of Englond
Edward, by the grace of
umble servant, William
yow peas, helthe, joye,
t and redoubted prynce.
t ye are enclined unto
, his nobles, lordes and
that ye sawe gladly the
prouffitable and honeste
of your hows, habound-
Therefore I have put
to myn handes, out of
tes, dictes and stories of
er wyse men, which ben
que wele, as well of the
d playe of the chesse,
l, I have made in the
on, not presumyng to
e ; for, God be thanked,
regions, as within the
oure and laud, whyche
other of what estate and
k, that they governed
t dere redoubted lord, I
gne to reseyve this lityll
humble and unknowen
n, for the right good
best wise I can, ought
clerely to procede in this

~~Mr. Mansell is very particular in ascribing to him Bartholomeus de proprietatib. first transla. & printed in English, 1471. but we have not been fortunate enough to meet wth it, as yet. Cat. p. 2. p. 13~~

See C.B. Harl. iij; No. 4048

1474.

WILLIAM CAXTON.

Mr. Bryant remarks ~~acquaints me~~ yt he has compared this Book wth ye Recueil des Histoires de Troyes, 1464, as well as wth ye Translation thereof by Caxton printed at Cologn 1471, and yt there is a perfect Resemblance between ym in ye manner of printing" for not only ye Page itself, but ye number of Lines in a Page, the length, breadth & intervals of ye lines are alike".

Bib. Har. No. 2296.

C.B.H. iij; 4048.

8. Does Caxton's printer's device conceal a date? Joseph Ames, *Typographical Antiquities*, 1749, annotated copy. British Library, C.60.o.5, p.5.

When in 1477 Caxton at last made a full statement about the date of printing of a book, it was of less importance to Ames, because in his view printing was by then well established in England. The book containing this statement was *The Dictes and Sayengs of the Philosophers*, also a translation from the French, but this time not by Caxton himself but by Anthony Woodville, Earl Rivers, who was closely connected with the court of Edward IV. Caxton wrote a long epilogue to Rivers' text which began by declaring that the book was printed in Westminster in 1477 (see Fig. 42). By a curious chance Ames knew the book in the only copy (out of about a dozen now known to survive) which has an additional colophon, printed at the end of Caxton's epilogue, which repeats that the book was printed in Westminster in 1477, but specifies the date of completion as 18 November (see Colour plate 1). Ames naturally assumed that this date applied to the whole edition, an assumption that we shall have to query.

In between the dates mentioned by Caxton in his earliest work, 1471, 1474 and 1477 (18 November) some twenty other books were gradually known to be printed by him. None of the other books bears any indication as to place or date of printing. The chances for endless discussion and rearrangement are obvious, and have not been missed.

AMES' CHRONOLOGICAL ARRANGEMENT

Ames was the first bibliographer to apply to Caxton's printing – in fact to apply to the work of any printer at all – a systematic approach which was much later to become part of the standard procedure in the study of incunabula. He distinguished the typefaces used by Caxton, reproduced specimens of them, and established that the *Recuyell* and *The Game of Chess* were printed in the same type. *The Dictes of the Philosophers* was printed in a different typeface, which is found in many other books. As, according to Ames' surmise the *Dictes* was printed later than the *Recuyell*, he called the *Recuyell*-type 'Type 1' and the typeface of *Dictes* 'Type 2'. But even with this rough division into earlier and later books there was not much of a basis for argument, nor were arguments always fully presented. Ames stated, for example, that he thought that the first edition of Chaucer's *Canterbury Tales* was printed by Caxton in 1475 or 1476. In this statement, followed by some others in the eighteenth century, he has proved to have been remarkably correct. The proof, however, was not made public until over 230 years later. Ames may well have based this dating on an observation that would have been possible in his time and is correct to this day, but since he did not set out his reasons, his dating of the *Canterbury Tales* was later forgotten.

Herbert and Dibdin retreated from Ames' standpoint that the first book printed in England was *The Game of Chess* with the date 1474. The conclusion, based on the great quantity of information and on the bibliographical pioneering work of the eighteenth century, accumulated in the studies of Ames, Herbert and Dibdin, was that Caxton first worked somewhere on the continent, perhaps before 1468, that by 1477 printing was established in Westminster, and that the date of transition was unknown. Not a bad record for the Age of Enlightenment.

9. Caxton's printer's device, first used in 1487.

William Blades

After a period of such sustained bibliographical activity there was a pause. Caxton's fame remained static for some time. The details of his life had reached an accepted form, and they were repeated thus in handbooks on early printing. Copies of his books continued to change hands, arousing the varying interest and commanding the varying prices that are the lot of antiquarian books. Renewed interest rose from a different quarter.

William Blades (1824–1890) was born in Clapham, the son of a printer, and destined to become a partner in the family firm of Blades & East. At the age of sixteen he was apprenticed at his father's firm in Abchurch Lane and in due course he and his brother directed the firm under the style of Blades, East & Blades. When William Blades turned his attention to Caxton he viewed the books in the first place with an expert typographer's eye. At the time when his interest in Caxton began, in the middle of the nineteenth century, the old craft of printing with a wooden press was rapidly dying out as the British inventions of the steam-driven press and its successors took over. Blades' enthusiasm was therefore generated by a mixture of pride in technological development and sentiment for the earlier craftsmanship. It proved to be highly infectious. Blades undertook the task of writing a new biography and bibliography of Caxton on a large scale, and did not hesitate to engage the help of others, more expert in certain fields. This broad approach was well rewarded.

Blades started his studies around 1855 and worked systematically; he examined all copies of all Caxton's books that he could possibly reach, and made a careful inventory of all the typographical material. To this end he had lithographic facsimiles prepared by G. I. F. Tupper, who patiently made an analysis of each of Caxton's typefaces, letter by letter, by going carefully through all the books (see Fig. 10). In this way development and changes in the printing types were noted, none of which had been observed before. This differentiation gave the chronological arrangement of Caxton editions a much firmer basis.

THE INFLUENCE OF H. BRADSHAW AND J. W. HOLTROP

In the course of examining all major collections which contained Caxton's work, Blades corresponded with and made the personal acquaintance of several librarians, who were more expert than he was

10. Lithograph-facsimile of the complete typecase of Caxton's Type 2 by G. I. F. Tupper, in William Blades, *The Life and Typography of William Caxton*. 2 vols., London 1861–63, vol. ii, Plate XIII.

in the purely bibliographical side of the matter. One of these men had a decisive influence. This was Henry Bradshaw, Librarian of Cambridge University and the most original and brilliant mind engaged on the history of the book in the last century, or perhaps ever. Bradshaw strongly encouraged Blades in his systematic approach. In fact he was not altogether satisfied with its rigour (however, he was seldom satisfied with any work he had influenced); and most importantly, he broadened Blades' horizon by directing him to the early printing of the Low Countries. One of Bradshaw's preoccupations at the time was how to cope with the massive quantity of information on printing in the Netherlands that had come to light with the secularization of monastic institutions at the time of Napoleon. Vast collections had come into private hands; their contents became known in the course of the nineteenth century as they changed hands and appeared in sale catalogues. In a similar fashion early English books had come to light in the eighteenth century; but in the Netherlands the number of incunable editions involved was much larger. The bibliographer who was studying the early printing of the Low Countries at that time was J. W. Holtrop, Librarian of the Royal Library in The Hague. As a step towards establing a systematic method of identification of early books he was publishing a series of facsimiles of all the printing types used in the Low Countries in the fifteenth century. Bradshaw and Holtrop, who both sought to bring discipline and order into the study of the history of printing, and exchanged ideas about methodology, can together be called the founding fathers of the modern study of incunabula. Bradshaw held that printing could not be studied in national isolation, and thus it was under his guidance that Blades turned his attention to the continent.

CAXTON AND COLARD MANSION

Here Blades was rewarded with his most important discovery. His experienced printer's eye detected a resemblance between the printing in red which occurs in Caxton's early books, and the red as printed in Bruges by a printer named Colard Mansion from 1476 on. This two-colour printing, a rather clumsy attempt at printing red and black at one pull which occurs in the work of both printers, suggested to Blades a common origin. If this defect was sufficient evidence of it, this one observation would provide answers to many of the questions accompanying Caxton's earliest group of books. Colard Mansion, who was known as the head of a workshop which produced luxurious manuscripts, would have printed these books in Bruges as a business deal with Caxton after Caxton had returned from Cologne. After Caxton's departure from Bruges, Mansion would have continued independently as a printer from 1476 on. Ironically, this daring theory failed to overcome the critical spirit of the two greatest experts, Holtrop and Bradshaw, under whose influence it had been formulated. Holtrop did not include the earliest Caxton types in his *Corpus* of types used in the Netherlands, and Bradshaw, after initial enthusiasm, placed the group of early Caxtons in the *'salle d'attente'* as he put it, waiting for further evidence.

But Blades' theory found wide acceptance in less critical hands,

38

obeying the rule that if a shaky theory is repeated frequently enough with increasing emphasis, it will convince the masses. And to be fair, no evidence has so far emerged to disprove it; indeed, there is now a good deal of circumstantial evidence to corroborate it, and it has found general acceptance. But there is no direct proof. And it is still open to question whether this is the *whole* truth.

BLADES' VIEW OF THE INTRODUCTION OF PRINTING INTO ENGLAND

On this basis Blades presented the beginning of English printing as having taken place in Bruges. He listed five books as printed in Bruges in Type 1, and he considered the *Recuyell* as the first of the Bruges books, probably completed in the year 1474. To *The Game of Chess*, which, as we have seen, bears the date 31 March 1474, he assigned a date in the year 1475 on the grounds that according to the French year style (whereby the year began at Easter) the date should be interpreted as 1475 since in that year Easter fell on 10 April. Moreover, he was of the opinion that the date 31 March applied to the translation, but that printing would have been completed not long after. The last book printed in Bruges would have been the *Cordiale*, a devout treatise on the Four Last Things which enjoyed massive popularity on the Continent. Caxton printed a translation into French. It contains red printing and it is set in Type 2, here probably used for the first time. Caxton would have moved to Westminster in 1476. The first book of substance to appear in Westminster was, according to Blades, *The History of Jason*, translated by Caxton and dedicated to the Prince of Wales. This was followed by *The Dictes of the Philosophers* with the date 18 November 1477. He therefore could assign to the *Jason* a date some time earlier in 1477. Blades was aware of the fact that only one copy of the *Dictes* bears the full date, in an additional colophon below the end of the text, while in several copies known to him this colophon is omitted altogether. He examined the copy with the more extensive statement, and was convinced that the colophon was printed at one pull with the rest of the page. This would mean that the type of the page was still standing, and in the fifteenth century this would certainly imply that there would have been no interval of time between the printing of the full edition of the sheet without colophon, and the sheet or sheets containing the addition. The date 18 November 1477 would therefore apply to the whole edition, and Blades attached great significance to it as the first date connected with printing in Westminster.

The impressive results of Blades' work were published by himself in two volumes, *The Life and Typography of William Caxton*, which appeared in 1861 and 1863. In it Blades provided the image in which the nation gladly accepted its arch-typographer. Here was the mercer from the Weald of Kent, brought up in London, who after his apprenticeship was enterprising enough to settle overseas and seek his fortune in the Flemish cloth trade. After years of relative obscurity he gradually rose to eminence. He became Governor of the English Nation, the settlement of English merchants in Bruges, and was shown to display all kinds of activity in representing English interests, and even to negotiate on behalf of the king in the many feuds between England and the Burgundian state. This enterprising merchant suddenly decided to embark on an entirely new venture and to make use of new technical developments that had come to his notice in order to spread literary and other works. He started this new career at what must have been a fairly advanced age for that time, when he had achieved a position of his own in very exalted circles.

Caxton's books were attractive, and his typographical material was beautifully presented by Blades in Tupper's lithographs. Blades combined this with other stylish illustrative material, and thereby succeeded in bringing Caxton both as a printer and as an individual much closer to an interested public.

THE CAXTON CELEBRATIONS OF 1877

After his publication Blades' own interest waned, as other commitments took over. His authority, however, grew with the popularity of his work. When plans arose for a celebration of the quatercentenary of the introduction of printing into England to be held at the end of 1877, a date based on the colophon in the *Dictes*, Blades naturally became its leader and organizer. The mantle of authority suited him. The fact that he left a posthumous work entitled *The Pentateuch of Printing* is not without significance. The celebrations of 1877 left their mark in various forms. A popular abbreviated version of Blades' book was published, which saw several reprints. There were numerous minor celebrations and there is a trail of stained-glass windows in which Caxton is assigned a patriarchal countenance. However, the culmination for which the quatercentenary is now remembered was a gigantic exhibition held in the South Kensington Museum (nowadays the Victoria and Albert Museum), which was mainly due to the joint efforts of Blades and of George Bullen, Keeper of Printed Books at the British Museum. The printed book, both in its early and in its most modern mechanically produced form was displayed on a scale and in a variety which was hitherto unheard of. It was a highly appropriate celebration of technology applied to the spread of knowledge.

40

11. Indulgence printed by Caxton in 1476. This, the only known copy, was issued by a priest at Westminster on 13 December 1476. He filled in the place and date by hand. London, Public Record Office, Exchequer K. R. Ecclesiastical Documents 6/56.

The Caxton celebrations in 1976

Ninety-nine years later a nation that had learnt in the meantime to value its freedom of the press gave thanks in Westminster Abbey for half a millennium of printing and celebrated this event throughout the land. The fact that these celebrations took place in 1976 and not a year later was due to new discoveries which had been made since Blades' time. At the end of the nineteenth century Dr Edward J. L. Scott, Keeper of the Muniments of Westminster Abbey, found a lease that showed that from Michaelmas 1476 on Caxton rented *una shopa* — apparently some sort of shop or workspace — from the sacrist and abbot. The document was known to E. Gordon Duff, a bibliographer who specialized in early printing in England. Duff wrote several studies of Caxton and of Westminster printing culminating in a bibliography of all English printing in the fifteenth century published in 1917. Although he mentioned the lease and quoted it briefly in 1905, Duff did not attach a great deal of significance to it, as he left out any mention of it in later Caxton studies. He did not regard it as proof of any activities of Caxton as printer in 1476.

In 1928, however, a piece of indubitable Westminster printing

41

bearing the date 1476 was brought to light in the Public Record Office. It was not a printed date, but the handwritten date of issue of a printed indulgence, filled in by a priest when he sold the document at Westminster to Henry Langley and his wife Katherine from Essex on 13 December 1476 (see Fig. 11). Thereby the *Dictes*, with its date 18 November 1477, lost its position of eminence as the earliest dated document connected with printing in Westminster.

Once the Indulgence was discovered, the date of the Westminster lease (Michaelmas, 29 September 1476) grew in significance. The document was at last published by W. J. B. Crotch in a collection of archival material concerning Caxton which served as an extensive preliminary to a text edition of Caxton's own prologues and epilogues to his books. Crotch's view of the earliest printing in England was founded on the dates both of the Westminster lease and the Indulgence, but did not conflict with that of Blades. According to this view, Caxton would have moved into his workshop in the Abbey precincts on 29 September 1476 and started preparations to instal himself as a printer. By early December 1476 he would have proceeded well enough with building his presses, preparing type, getting supplies of paper and ink, and organizing his workmen to produce some modest specimens of ephemeral printing of which only the (now famous) Indulgence survives.

Hence the Caxton celebrations of 1976 reached their peak towards the end of September, for that was clearly the time of the year when Caxton's arrival in England should be commemorated.

THE DATING OF THE FIRST LEASE

It was an expression of tact on the part of the Librarian of Westminster Abbey, Howard M. Nixon, to postpone publication of his careful reassessment of the Westminster documents until December 1976, when the celebrations were well over. For his findings cast an initial doubt (which has grown since then) on the validity of the assumption that it was in September 1476 that Caxton's printing shop came into existence. By placing the documents in their context of other contemporary archival records, Nixon demonstrated that the *shopa* was not likely to have been the only accommodation rented by Caxton in the Abbey precincts, nor that it housed his workshop. It is altogether more probable that the printing house was established in the Almonry in a house named The Red Pale. Caxton can be shown by entries in the Prior's accounts to have paid a quarterly rent to the Prior for this house from 1482 on. However, we also know that Caxton gave the Red Pale as his address when he advertised his *Ordinale* for sale: '. . . late hym come to westmonester in to the almonesrye at the reed pale . . .' (see Fig. 12).

42

We shall discuss the date of printing of the *Ordinale* and its advertisement later on, but nobody has any doubt that this took place well before 1482. The absence of a record before 1482 for the house in the Almonry does not mean, as Nixon pointed out, that Caxton did *not* rent The Red Pale. There are no Prior's records at all extant from 1456 until records began again in 1482. There is therefore no way to know when Caxton first rented The Red Pale. Nixon's observation invalidates the importance of the rental of the *shopa* as positively marking the beginning in Westminster, for Caxton could have started to pay rent for The Red Pale at any time before September 1476. In fact, as we shall see, it is not likely to have been much earlier. Nonetheless the date of Michaelmas (29 September) 1476 has lost its assumed significance.

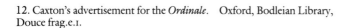

12. Caxton's advertisement for the *Ordinale*.   Oxford, Bodleian Library, Douce frag.e.1.

Research in the years between 1877 and 1976

The quincentenary celebrations were an occasion for reassessment and summarizing of what had been known before. A good deal of literature had come into existence since Blades' *Life and Typography*. More was published than can be related here, or even be mentioned in passing, as we wish to concentrate here only on the short period of the introduction of printing into England. Excellent biographies were published during the quincentenary year in which all the known facts of Caxton's life before and after the short episode when he settled in Westminster can be found. Archival documents had been found in the century preceding the quincentenary, known facts had been re-interpreted; and unknown editions had come to light in forgotten volumes in half-forgotten libraries. Nowadays unrecorded Caxtons tend rather to turn up as snippets of indulgences or even of books, folded away in early bindings. Nothing has proved to be more evasive than two editions of the *Sarum Hours*, quite unknown but for the ghostly offsets of some of their pages on a piece of printer's waste of a collection of prayers, called *The Fifteen Oes*, stuck in an early Caxton binding. They were recognized for what they are by George D. Painter, who patiently studied their reflexion in a mirror, and they now take up a very special position in the incunable collection of the British Library. Thanks to optical aids it is now possible to read the offsets somewhat more easily than by peering into a mirror. The reversed image as seen on the screen of a 'Visualtek' reader is shown in Fig. 14.

INSIDE CAXTON'S WORKSHOP: HIS COMPOSITORS DETECTED AT WORK

The central issue of this study is the introduction of printing into England and its significance; on this matter the discovery of new editions and the establishment of an ever clearer picture of Caxton's printed output has a direct bearing. Another discovery also helps us to understand how Caxton's printing house worked, although its relevance is not immediately obvious. We shall discuss it briefly.

Monsignor José Ruysschaert published in 1953 his discovery of a manuscript in Latin used by Caxton's compositors as printer's copy (as an example, or *exemplar* to use the technical term). It is a very valuable document to have, for it brings us close to the way a book was made in Caxton's printing house in its early years. Printer's copy enables us to follow compositors in their work because it was

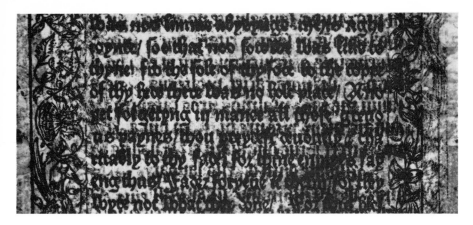

13. Detail from a fragment of Caxton's *The Fifteen Oes* with offsets of otherwise unknown Books of Hours.   British Library, IA. 55144 a.

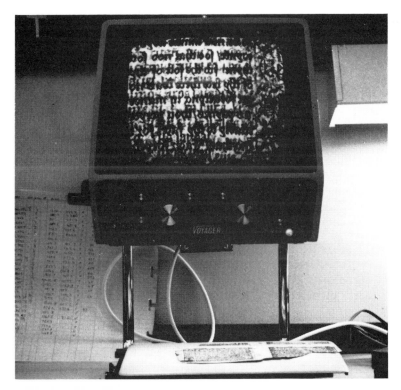

14. Reversed image of the same fragment, photographed from a Visualtek screen.

circumscribed by technical requirements and limitations. Their many small decisions, taken as they went along, determined the final form of a text in its printed version.

The manuscript which Ruysschaert studied (which is preserved in the Vatican Library) has the title *Nova Rhetorica* or *Margarita Eloquentie*. The text was written by the learned Franciscan friar Laurentius Traversanus who travelled in Italy, Austria, France and Flanders, teaching wherever he went, and who had stayed in England in the years 1476–1478. The *Nova Rhetorica* was completed in Cambridge on 26 July 1478. Ruysschaert noticed in the manuscript, which was written by the author, the occurrence of figures and dashes in a certain pattern. The text was printed by Caxton late in 1478 or early in 1479, and the figures correspond with the beginning of pages in Caxton's printed edition. Ruysschaert concluded therefore that the manuscript had been the example used by Caxton's compositors (see Fig. 15).

15. Manuscript of Laurentius Traversanus, *Nova Rhetorica*, used in Caxton's workshop. The figure 10, the wriggle at the end of a line and the dividing line are marks made by the compositor, to mark the beginning of the tenth page in quire 0.   Biblioteca Apostolica Vaticana, Cod.lat.11441.

The figures and dashes are signs of 'casting off'. This is the calculation of pages before the typesetting of each quire, a procedure which is necessary in order to combine pages that are to be printed on one side of a sheet which are put together to make up a 'forme'. In the case of the *Nova Rhetorica*, an edition printed in folio format, a forme was made up by putting two pages together. The figures indicated the page numbers within the quires as planned ahead. The little dashes were markings made by the compositors to indicate in the manuscript where they had come to the end of their typeset pages. Their page-end could differ from the casting off. Later they would continue setting the following page at the exact spot marked in the manuscript, but they would not necessarily continue immediately after typesetting the previous page. Other pages might have to be completed first in order to finish the forme or the typesetting and printing of the sheet. This is because the supply of type was limited; at that time there was always less type available than in later centuries. Not until the mid-seventeenth century was a book normally set in the order in which the text could be read in the *exemplar*, for setting a book in textual order meant that a large stretch of it had to wait standing in type before a quire could be printed.

The *Nova Rhetorica* is, so far, the only manuscript that has been recognized as having served as printer's copy in Caxton's workshop. The *Rhetorica* was an exceptional work for Caxton's men since it was in Latin. Caxton's compositors would have shown more understanding and probably more freedom towards a text in their native language. In this case their unease and inaccuracy is most revealing, although there are also some errors in the manuscript which are correct in the text as printed while there is no mark in the manuscript to show any interference by an editor. Typesetting was by no means an automatic process. We have to keep this observation in mind when we are looking at Caxton's edition of Malory's *Le Morte Darthur*.

DISCOVERY OF THE COLOGNE RECORD: CAXTON'S EARLY CAREER

As we have already seen, the combination of archival documents and printed material can be particularly illuminating, and provide irrefutable evidence. In the course of this century much more light was thrown on the earliest part of Caxton's printing career. Documents on Caxton's sojourn in Cologne indicate the precise date of its beginning and end. They were first brought to the notice of the English public in 1924 by a British officer, Colonel J. G. Birch, after this information had spent a long period of incubation in a footnote in an edition of Hanseatic records, *Hansisches Urkundenbuch*, published in Leipzig in 1907. The Cologne records were reinterpreted by Professor Severin Corsten in 1976, and his interpretation is followed here. Caxton obtained permission from the authorities in Cologne to stay there from 17 July 1471, and from several renewals it appears that he stayed until Christmas 1472 without interruption. This fits in with Caxton's own statements in *The Recuyell of the Historyes of Troye* where the date 19 September 1471 is given for the completion of the translation in Cologne. It also suggests a date early in 1473 for his return to Flanders.

In the meantime the date 31 March 1474 found at the end of *The Game of Chess* had acquired a new significance due to the work of Professor N. F. Blake, who finally did away with the confusion concerning this date created by William Blades. Blades had argued that 31 March 1474 had to be interpreted in the Easter style as 1474/75, as Easter fell in 1474 on 10 April. However, nobody before Professor Blake had observed that in the year 1475 Easter fell on 26 March and that therefore, according to the Easter style, the date '31 March 1474' (i.e. 1474/75) was a date which could not have existed. Moreover Blake argued that there was no reason to expect that an English book dedicated to the Duke of Clarence would be dated according to the Easter style. In Westminster the year began on Lady Day (25 March) if the secular year, beginning on 1 January, was not followed. The date 31 March 1474 should therefore be read at its face value. Professor Blake also demonstrated on linguistic grounds that the date is more likely to apply to the completion of printing than to that of the translation. If *The Game of Chess* was completed on 31 March 1474, the period from early 1473 to early 1474 is left in which Caxton could have organized a printing house, and printed *The Recuyell of the Historyes of Troye*, unanimously considered, in accordance with Caxton's own testimony, to be the first book printed by him in English. There is still no absolute certainty as to its place of printing – perhaps Bruges, as for *The Game of Chess* and the later books, or somewhere else in Flanders? — but as to its dating we are now on much firmer ground.

The *Recuyell* and *The Game of Chess* together contain 426 leaves or 213 sheets. A printing house, working smoothly with one press and producing on average one edition sheet on each working day, would require between nine and ten months to complete this amount of work. The *Recuyell* was probably printed on two presses working concurrently. The fifteen months between the beginning of 1473 and the end of March 1474 would therefore be a realistic length of time for Caxton to have started his enterprise and produced the first two books, if he had the efficient support which there is every reason to assume he had. The total number of sheets of the other Bruges books now known, all printed later than *The Game of Chess* and all undated, amounts to 265 or about 285 sheets (depending on what place of printing is assigned to the first edition of the *Sarum Hours*). One year contained about 260 working days, excluding the Sundays and feast days of obligation when work for financial gain was not permitted. Caxton's later output in Bruges would have required therefore a little over a year of organized, regular work. This would bring us to the summer of 1475.

Dyctes & sayengis a parte in thende of this book, to thentent
that yf my sayd lord or ony other persone What someuer he
or she be that shal rede or here it, that If they be not Wel
plesyd Wyth all that they Wyth a penne race it out or el-
lys rente the leef out of the booke, Humbly requyryng and
besechyng my sayd lord to take no displaysir on me so presumyng but to pardone Where as he shal fynde faulte, and
that it plese hym to take the labour of thenpryntyng in gre
& thanke, Whiche gladly haue don my dyligence in thaccom-
plysshyng of his desire and commandement. In Why
che I am bounden so to do for the good reward that I haue resseyuyd of his sayd lordship, Whom I beseche Al-
myghty god tencrece and to contynue in his vertuous dis-
posicion in this World, And after thys lyf to lyue euer-
lastyngly in heuen Amen

Et sic est finis

Thus endeth this book of the dyctes and notable Wyse sayenges of the phylosophers late translated and drawen
out of frensshe into our englisshe tonge by my forsaid lord
Therle of Ryuers and lord Skales, and by hys comandement sette in forme and emprynted in this manere as
ye maye here in this booke see Whiche Was fynisshed the
xviij day of the moneth of Nouembre, & the seuententh
yere of the regne of kyng Edward the fourth.

1. *The Dictes of the Philosophers*: the added colophon survives in only one
copy.   Manchester, John Rylands University Library, Inc.15542, leaf [k]4 verso.

Ẽie begynneth the volume intitued and named the recuyell of the historyes of Troye, composed and drawen out of dyuerce bookes of latyn in to frensshe by the ryght venerable persone and worshipfull man: Raoul le ffeure, preest and chapelayn vnto the ryght noble gloryous and myghty prynce in his tyme Phelip duc of Bourgoyne of Braband. &c. In the yere of the Incarnacion of our lord god a thousand foure honderd sixty and foure / And translated and drawen out of frensshe into englissh by Willyam Caxton mercer of ye cyte of London / at the comaundemet of the right hye myghty and vertuouse Pryncesse hys redoubtyd lady: Margarete by the grace of god Duchesse of Bourgoyne of Lotryk of Braband. &c. / Whiche sayd translacion and werke was begonne in Brugis in the Countee of Flaundres the fyrst day of marche the yere of the Incarnacion of our sayd lord god a thousand foure honderd sixty and eyghte / And ended and fynysshid in the holy cyte of Coleyn the. xix. day of septembre the yere of our sayd lord god a thousand foure honderd sixty and enleuen. &c.

And on that other syde of this leef foloweth the prologe

11. Caxton's opening words for the first book printed in English, *The Recuyell of the Historyes of Troye*, giving dates of beginning and completion of his translation. British Library, C.11.c.1, leaf [a] 2 recto.

Once the exact period of Caxton's lengthy stay in Cologne had been determined, it became possible to gain a better insight into his typography. From the beginning, Caxton's bibliographers had accepted his own statement that he had learned the craft of printing 'at his great charge and dispense' in the city of Cologne. In the eighteenth century a corroboration of this statement was found in a book printed by Caxton's successor Wynkyn de Worde, at the end of the English translation of Bartholomaeus Anglicus', *De proprietatibus rerum*. Wynkyn de Worde added a long reflective poem about the contents of the book as he had published it, much in the manner of Caxton's epilogues.

He included the lines:

> And also of your charyte call to remembraunce
> The soule of William Caxton first prynter of this boke
> In laten tonge at Coleyn hymself to avaunce
> That every well disposyd man may theron loke . . . .

16. Bartholomaeus Anglicus, *De proprietatibus rerum* (in English), Westminster, Wynkyn de Worde, *c*.1495. British Library, G.10565, leaf oo 5 recto, (detail).

It took a long time before any edition of Bartholomaeus Anglicus in Latin was recognized as having anything to do with Caxton, although such an edition does exist. Its typographical appearance is that of the books printed in Cologne in that period, which bears no resemblance at all to the books printed by Caxton (see Fig. 17).

Now, however, a developing insight into the structure of early printing and publishing in Cologne, and of printing in the Netherlands, combined to bring one figure to the fore. This was Johannes Veldener, a versatile typographer, who began his career in the

49

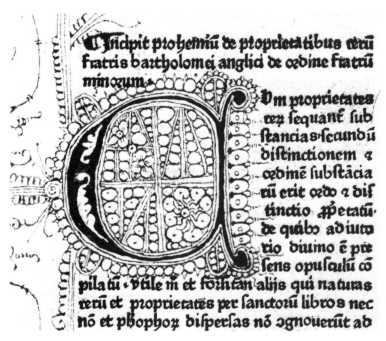

17. Bartholomaeus Anglicus, *De proprietatibus rerum*. Cologne, Printer of the *Flores Sancti Augustini* (William Caxton?), *c.*1472. British Library, IC.3771, leaf [a] 1 recto, (detail).

printing business in Cologne where he must have designed types for several printers, whom he may also have assisted in other ways. He was probably commissioned by Caxton to print the Bartholomaeus Anglicus (and possibly other related books) at the same time instructing him in the arts of printing and managing a printing house. Veldener's name did not appear in print until after he had left Cologne and started to work independently in Louvain, in 1475. One of the typefaces in an unfinished version, used by him in that year for chapter-headings, next appeared in its definitive state in Caxton's books (see Fig. 18). It was used for the last books printed in Bruges (the French *Cordiale* and perhaps the *Sarum Hours*) and subsequently it was Caxton's most important type in the early Westminster years. It is the typeface designated as 'Caxton Type 2', as it succeeded the typeface used in the *Recuyell* and most of the other books connected with the Bruges period.

Veldener's appearance in the history of Caxton's career by no means eclipsed Colard Mansion, but it rather had the effect of confirming Mansion's role – which had been emphasized in different ways by several bibliographers since Blades – as the man who, with

Caxton's backing, began to produce 'mechanically written' books in the atelier where he had hitherto specialized in fine manuscripts. Veldener certainly provided Type 2 and probably cut also Caxton's rather curious first type according to the instructions of the novice publisher. He must have taught Mansion, or rather Mansion's scribes, how to copy a text in metal type instead of with pen and ink and, as they continued typesetting the pages of their first book, to print them in as many copies as were required 'all at once', an everyday miracle which still astonished Caxton when the end of the *Recuyell* was reached, as appears from the words of his epilogue. By the time Caxton left Bruges for Westminster, Veldener had begun work on what was to become Caxton Type 3, a type that was going to enjoy great popularity with a number of printers, both in the Low Countries and in England.

Perhaps, delighted as they were by the emerging picture, some of Caxton's most recent historians may have exaggerated Veldener's part in Caxton's later career as printer by postulating that Veldener furnished most of the types used by Caxton until the end of his active life. However this may be, it is certain that Veldener's presence was decisive for the form of Caxton's publications in Bruges and in the first years in Westminster. The growing knowledge of printing in Cologne and the Netherlands has brought this hidden fact to light.

18. A preliminary state of Caxton's Type 2 used by Johannes Veldener for titles in Angelus de Gambilionibus, *Lectura super titulo de actionibus*, Louvain, 1475. Cambridge, University Library, Oates 3687, leaf [a] 1 recto.

Present research for the Catalogue of incunabula in the British Library

The present state of research into the introduction of printing into England is unconnected with celebrations, a circumstance that may free the mind from a preoccupation with dates. It is part of a work that has been growing since the beginning of this century, the *Catalogue of books printed in the XVth. Century now in the British Museum*, a title usually abbreviated to BMC. The collection of incunabula that used to be part of the library of the British Museum, (and which since 1973 has belonged to the British Library), is one of the largest and most important collections in the world. Its printed catalogue, which goes into great descriptive detail, follows the progress of printing through Europe, and is arranged by country, city and then by printer. It starts in Germany in the city of Mainz, where the history of modern printing began with the inventions of Johannes Gutenberg in the 1450s. It follows the spread of printing through Germany, from city to city until the end of the fifteenth century. It then goes back to the year 1465 to the beginning of printing in Italy in Subiaco and Rome, and from there on to Venice, Florence and the many other Italian cities where printing flourished. From Italy the catalogue picks up the trail again in France, where printing started in 1470 at the Sorbonne. From France it goes on to the Low Countries, and it is there (by now we have arrived at volume ix) that it first had to deal with Caxton (having allotted him some very small print in Cologne) when the early Bruges books were described. But before the catalogue could go on with Caxton's career in England it had to cover Spain and Portugal, where printing was introduced around 1473. The Spanish volume was completed in 1970 and the volume dealing with England is the next one due. The collection of English incunabula is proportionally even more representative of printing in the fifteenth century than any other part of the collection: hence the extra attention given to it.

Preparations for volume xi started as early as 1950, with George D. Painter as editor. He worked concurrently on the Netherlands and the Iberian Peninsula, which had to come out first. Painter gave a permanent form to part of this work in his biography of Caxton which appeared in 1976. In this book he attempts to integrate the history of Caxton-the-individual and Caxton-the-printer into the known historical events of his time, which was of course one of the most turbulent episodes in British history. Once again it was Caxton who was chosen as the subject of a pioneering effort in bibliographical scholarship. In an age where the integration of specialist knowledge into related fields (in this case the history of the book into political and literary history) is one of the main problems of scholarship, the influence of Painter's book is bound to be felt for a long time.

A catalogue, however, requires a different emphasis. The books, not their printer, are the central issue, and their relationship and arrangement are the overriding questions. After Painter's retirement from the Library the present author became editor of BMC-England; and shortly afterwards Dr Paul Needham, Curator of Printed Books at the Pierpont Morgan Library in New York, who had for some time been studying the paper used by Caxton, was appointed to the Library as honorary consultant on paper studies and as co-editor of BMC-England.

Now it was possible to combine the study of paper with typographical research in order to reach a new chronological arrangement. Two independent lines of evidence, provided they achieve results that can be reconciled with each other, vastly improve the support for any theory. Moreover, experience proved that typography sometimes could provide clues for paper researches, and vice-versa. It is therefore difficult – and unnecessary – to establish the priority of either one or the other.

Bibliographers had tried to use paper as evidence for identification of books ever since the eighteenth century. They had always run into difficulties because tracings of watermarks are not sufficient to make a precise distinction between paper-stocks, a distinction which only becomes apparent through slight differences in position and shape of the marks and their relation to the wires of the moulds in which paper was made. Only after the arrival in the 1960s of beta-

19. Beta-radiograph. Paper marked with a mermaid was used in English printing in 1480.

radiography, a process which produces photographic negatives of the image of the paper without showing the writing or printing on its surfaces, did a sufficiently accurate method become available to establish full records of the paper-stocks used by a printer. All the papers used within a printing-house can now accurately be distinguished, their successive or concurrent use at the presses can be followed, and links between editions can be established. (Fig. 19.)

The history of typography had also undergone renewal. Bibliographical discipline requires that types be distinguished and classified in order to establish the chronological sequences of printing-types or books. Under the influence of typographical historians such as Stanley Morison and Harry Carter there is now the further inclination to look beyond the type as it was printed on the page. We seek to identify and to categorise a type in relation to other types, and to ask such questions as: who designed and cut it, who owned the punches, who had matrices, where was it cast and was it recast? In trying to find answers to these questions we discover the ramifications of the trade in typographical material and relations between printers; this understanding contributes towards a more accurate chronology.

THE FIRST TWENTY BOOKS PRINTED AT WESTMINSTER

With this renewed application of old techniques we approached the question of the chronology of Caxton's earliest Westminster books. So far these have been mentioned only sketchily: they must now be listed in somewhat greater detail.

The earliest date for Westminster printing is, as we have seen, that in the Indulgence bearing the manuscript date 13 December 1476. Generally the first major books were thought to be *The History of Jason* followed by *The Dictes of the Philosophers* on 18 November 1477. Last came the largest book of all, the *Canterbury Tales*. There were also fourteen small books all printed in quarto, some of which were thought to have preceded *Jason*, but most would have been printed concurrently with the larger books. Finally there was the *Ordinale*, also known as the *Sarum Pie*, printed in quarto, once a sizeable volume but surviving in only a few leaves. For this book, which provided instructions for the observation of feast days, Caxton printed an advertisement. Caxton used two printing types for these books, Type 2 and Type 3, and it is useful to take note of them at this stage. Early in 1479 a recasting of Type 2 was introduced. Printing before that date, in which Type 2 occurs in its first state, can be listed in the traditional order as follows:

54

(before		
13 December 1476)	*Indulgence*	Type 2 + 3
(1477)	*The History of Jason*	Type 2 + 3
(1477)	11 books in quarto	Type 2
(1477/78)	3 books in quarto	Type 2 + 3
18 November 1477	*The Dictes of the Philosophers*	Type 2 + 3
20 February 1478	*Moral Proverbs*	Type 2 + 3
(1478)	*Canterbury Tales*	Type 2
(1478)	*Boethius*	Type 2 + 3
(thereafter)	*Ordinale* with Advertisement	Type 3

It will at once be clear that this chronological sequence can only be accepted on the assumption that Caxton arrived in Westminster with Type 2 fully available (it had in fact been used in Bruges), and at least enough of Type 3 to supplement Type 2. Naturally these books can be divided into those printed with Type 2 alone, and those printed in a combination of Type 2 and Type 3. There is however an obstacle to attaching any chronological significance to this division. The very first word of the Indulgence (in this chronological sequence even the very first word printed in England) is the name (I)Ohannes, printed in Type 3. Only after the paper evidence had indicated a different chronological sequence for these books the simultaneous introduction of the two types had to be queried. Thereupon their relationship was better understood.

TWO VARIANT FORMS OF LETTERS: A TYPOGRAPHICAL CLUE

The key to this new sequence was not found directly in paper evidence, but in a combination of typographical and textual observations. Johannes Veldener had succeeded in creating in Type 2 a typeface of new and very original design. It was inspired by the style of the luxurious Burgundian manuscripts owned by princes and noblemen, adapted to an elegant typographical form of its own (see Fig. 20). The lofty, ceremonial style of the type may help us to understand some peculiarities in its use. For some letters it has two variant forms, something which may seem strange to us now, but which was not unknown in the fifteenth century. But what was unusual even then is the care with which the two forms of letters

55

Our counsel shal not longe be to seche
As thoughte it was not worth to make vs wyse
And graunted hym withoute more aduyse
And bad hym saye his verdit as hym list
Lordynges qd he now herkeneth for the best
But take it not I pray you in disdeyne
This is the poynt to speke it short & pleyne
That eche of you to shorte with your weye
In this viage shal telle talis tweye
To Cauntirburyward I mene it so
And homward he shal telle other talis to
Of auentuuris that whilom haue befalle
And whiche of you berith hym best of alle
That is to sey that tellith in this case
Tales of best sentence and most solace
Shal haue a soper of oure alther cost
Here in this place sittynge by this post
Whan that ye come ayen from Caunterbury
And forto make you the more mery
I wil my self go with you and ryde
Right at myn owen cost and be your gyde
And who that wol my iugement with say
Shortly shal paye all that is spent be the way
And if ye vouchesauf that it be soo
Tel me anone withoute wordis moo
And I wil hertly shape me therfore
This thing was graunted & othis swore
With ful glad herte & preyen hym also
That he wolde vouchesauf to do so

were distinguished. They had each a different value, and were assigned places of different order in the procession of letters that forms words and sentences. Protocol gave precedence to the wide and haughty ones, while the spindlier forms played a humbler part in the elaborate system. In fact what we see here is a typographer trying to avoid a decision familiar to all palaeographers of the present day: is this letter a capital or a minuscule? Typography as a medium is infinitely more restricted in graphic forms than script with its endless variety and ambiguity. Veldener experimented with an intermediate form, between capital and minuscule, a kind of compromise frequently encountered in script. But in the development of typographical forms simplification overruled subtlety, and the experiment was doomed.

One letter that had two shapes in Type 2 is the capital R. One form was narrow and is for us perhaps difficult to recognize as an R. It is very much in the tradition of the cursive Burgundian script. There is also a wide form of the letter in which we can at once see an R-shape. Caxton's compositors used the narrow R to do the ordinary work, in prose, while the wide one is found in verse, where its purpose is to signify the beginning of lines and to give extra emphasis (see Fig. 21). It is never seen in the middle of lines of

21. In Type 2 one form of R is found at the beginning of lines of verse, the other form in the middle. An example from the *Canterbury Tales*.   British Library, 167.c.26, leaf [o] 4 verso.

verse, where we find the narrow R. It was probably thought that the narrow R gave less of an interruption in the flow of language. It must be remembered, of course, that in the fifteenth century reading always meant reading aloud. When the eye was halted or diverted, the voice also paused. Graphic forms could therefore support the written or printed text in a function similar to that of a musical score.

This is how the use of two forms of I can also best be understood. There is a narrow, upright I, and there is a wide one with a fine sweeping flourish (see Fig. 22). The narrow I is normally used in prose, but the wide I is sometimes obviously used for the very

Shal Weddid be Vnto January
I trowe it were you to longe to tary
If I you tolde of every escrit and bond

22. In Type 2 the wide form of I is found at the beginning of lines of verse, the narrow I in the middle. From the *Canterbury Tales*.   British Library, 167.c.26, leaf [p] 5 verso.

purpose of interrupting the flow of language and of the voice. It demanded attention, and like punctuation it could be used to create a space, a pause to take a deep breath in preparation for extra rhetorical emphasis. It is strikingly used to this effect in the French *Cordiale*, printed in Bruges. At the Last Judgement the devil addresses the Almighty and implores Him to let him have possession of a soul:

'O tu juste juge, *Juge* le doncques estre mien et quil soit condempne a estre avec moy perpetuellement.'

('O thou, just judge, *Judge* then that he belongs to me and that he will be condemned to stay with me for ever.')

cy Semu about la mienne. O tu Juste Juge Juge le doncques estre mien et quil soit condempne a estre auec moy perpetuellement. Ces parolles dist nostreseigneur a saint

23. The *Cordiale* in French. The wide I is used for rhetorical emphasis. British Library, IB.49437, leaf. [c] 5 verso.

In the books of verse printed in Westminster we see that the wide I, as the wide R, is always used at the beginning of lines, and the narrow I in all other positions when a capital was required.

TWO FORMS OF *A*
LEAD TO TWO COMPOSITORS

Once we understand the hierarchy of the variant forms of letters, we are able to grasp what happened with one other variant letter-form, that of the *a*. There are two forms again, one with two storeys, the double **a**, and one simpler round **a**. When Type 2 was used in the *Cordiale* in Bruges, the double *a* was consistently used in every word beginning with a, and the round *a* in all other positions, in the middle and at the end of words (see Fig. 24). We see this also in one

24. The *Cordiale* in French. The double *a* is used at the beginning of words, the round *a* in all other positions. British Library, IB.49437, leaf [b] 4 recto.

other book printed in Type 2, the small *Sarum Hours*, in Latin (see Fig. 25), but in none of the twenty books that form Caxton's

25. *Horae ad usum Sarum.* Double *a* is used at the beginning of words. This fragment was taken from a binding. Oxford, Bodleian Library, Douce frag.g.1.1, leaves 2 verso, 3 recto.

Of thebes With his Wast Wallis Wyde
And Venus sletth me in that other syde
For Jelosie and feer of hym and arcite
Now Wol J stynte of Palamon alite
And lete hym in his prison stille duelle
And of arcite forth J Wol you telle
The somer passed the nyghtis Way long
Encreath he dubil Wyse the peynes strong
Bothe of the louer and of the prisoner
J ne Woot Who hath the Wofuller myster
For shortly to say of this Palamon
Perpetuelly is dampned to prison
In cheynps and in feters to be ded
And arcite is exiled on his hed
For euermore and out of that contre
For neuer more shal be his lady se
Now louers aye J now this question
Who hath the Worse of arcite & of Palamon
That one may se his lady day be day
But in prison muste he dwelle al Way
That other Where hym list may ryde or goo
But se his lady shal he neuer moo
Now demyth as ye list ye that can
For J Wil telle forth as J began
Whan that arcite to Thebes come Was
Ful ofte aday he sWelte and sayde allas
For se his lady shal he neuer moo
And shortly to conclude all his Woo
So moche sorow ne hath creature

26. The name *arcite*, which occurs five times on this page of the *Canterbury Tales* is
every time set with double *a*.   British Library, 167.c.26, leaf [c] 8 verso.

output in the first years in Westminster. When Type 2 was taken to Westminster, Caxton's new compositors, who were perfectly consistent in using the two forms of R and I according to the set of manners devised in Bruges, were apparently unfamiliar with the function of the two *a*'s in protocol.

Not every compositor used it in the same way. In fact, this is the most convenient way to distinguish the work of at least two compositors. One of them gave the double *a* the status of a kind of capital, of somewhat less importance than A. He used it in names as in the name *arcite* in the *Canterbury Tales*, (see Fig. 26) or in peculiar and obscure words, such as the titles of the learned books of the scholar Nicholas in the Miller's Tale, his mathematical handbooks, the *almegeste* and the *awgrym*, and his book on *astrology* (see

His almegeste his bokis grete and smale
His astrologye, longinge for his art
His algrym stones lay feire apart

27. The books of the scholar Nicholas in 'The Miller's Tale' get the double *a*. British Library, 167.c.26, leaf [g] 8 recto.

Fig. 27). Combined with punctuation it could indicate a pause, or the double *a*'s could merely reveal interesting nouns: *apostles, ambassador, alcoly, angels, apotecaryes, albification*, or words that attract a natural emphasis: *abhominacions, ale*. These examples were all taken from the first half of the *Canterbury Tales*. This use of the double *a* is not confined to the *Canterbury Tales* alone but it is by no means found in all twenty books. It occurs in some of the quarto editions, but hardly at all in the other folios.

In the second half of the *Canterbury Tales*, beginning with the larger section in prose, in most of *The History of Jason* and in the other folios, we encounter a very different use of the double *a*. Here the compositor seems to have tried to avoid the double *a* altogether. He may have disliked it, because stylistically the two-storeyed *a* does not belong to the Burgundian bastarda script from which Type 2 was developed. However, he did use it occasionally, but then in a way markedly different from what the first compositor of the *Canterbury Tales* did. He might use just a few double *a*'s very rarely and quite indifferently, probably because they had become mixed with the round *a*'s in the type-case. We find this in the prose section of the *Canterbury Tales* and in some of the small quartos. Also, shortage of type could force him to use double *a*'s. We can see this at the end of some pages of *The History of Jason* where the round *a* was used exclusively until the compositor suddenly ran out of them and used the double *a* for every single *a* regardless of position within the word (see Fig. 28). We find yet a further different use of the double *a* in the quarto-editions.

the way for to go vnto the kingꝫ . Whiche cam andꝫ yſſueꝺ out of his palais armeꝺꝫ andꝫ in poynt for tentre into bataiſſ . Thene he wente vnto the porte ꜩ cheſe out four honꝺerdꝫ of the beſte in poynt for to put into the ſaydꝫ four galeyes / Andꝫ fynably whan he haꝺꝫ doñ aſſ this he meuydꝫ fro the porte as ſaydꝫ is / andꝫ with aſſ haſte maꝺe his galeyes to be woweꝺꝫ after the knightes of grece / in ſuche wiſe as the maiſter marowner apperæyueꝺꝫ that the galeyes cam ſwifteſy after them for to feche agayn the fayr Medea + ꜩ calleꝺꝫ Jaſon that Japedꝫ ꜩ playedꝫ with medea / pſent his felawe hercules + ꜩ ſhewiꝺꝫ to him the four galeyes armeꝺꝫ where in was the kingꝫ Oetes andꝫ his men wel in poynt

28. The compositor of *The History of Jason* ran out of round *a*'s at the end of a page and used double *a*'s instead.   British Library, C.10.b.3, leaf [o] 6 recto.

CAXTON'S EARLY QUARTOS

Caxton's early quartos are all pretty little books, some containing texts for well-brought-up children, teaching good manners or a little Latin. Several of them contain some of the shorter poems by Chaucer and Lydgate. The few copies still extant survived in volumes which each contained a number of them together. Three titles were so successful that Caxton printed them twice, Lydgate's *The Horse, the Sheep and the Goose, The Churl and the Bird* and Benedict Burgh's translation of *Cato*.

The little books are very rare indeed. The British Library possesses only a few fragments, which had been used in a binding after they had been discarded in the printing house as waste-sheets. There is a fine set of these books in the University Library at Cambridge and several are in the Pierpont Morgan Library in New York. Traditionally the *Horse*, the *Churl* and the *Cato* in Cambridge were thought to be Caxton's first editions of these texts. There had been one dissenting voice some 40 years ago. The then Curator of Printed Books of the Pierpont Morgan Library, Dr C. F. Bühler, argued that the *Churl* in his collection was the earlier edition. His evidence was purely textual, and, perhaps because it was rather intricate, his reasoning went unheeded.

DISTINCTION OF COMPOSITORS

As editions the Cambridge and the Morgan books are hard to distinguish. One of them must be a careful copy of the other. Paul Needham, once alerted to the different use of the two *a*'s, did however observe that the distinction could find an application in establishing the order of the two editions of the *Horse, Sheep and Goose*. On the first page of the Cambridge book, for example, the compositor set the nouns *antiquite* and *auctorite* with a double *a*, but the word *audience*, six lines lower, escaped special notice and got the round *a*. In the copy in the Pierpont Morgan Library, *antiquite*, *auctorite* are set in the same way as in the Cambridge edition, but *audience* is set here with a double *a*, and therefore gets that slight extra emphasis that it lacks in the Cambridge book. At the end of both editions, after the end of Lydgate's poem, both books contain a long list of over a hundred collective nouns, 'A brase of houndes, a couple of spaniels, a flight of doves, a flock of sheep', etc. These are variations on the ways to designate a group of animals and were here seriously intended, while continuing the rustic theme of *The Horse, the Sheep and the Goose*, to explore the richness of the language, and also to extend the use of these terms more playfully to living things which normally would not be the subject of such categorisation:

a Slouth of beres   a Crase of ay hare
a Lees of grehoundes   Skulke of foxes
a Brase of houndes   a Skulke of freres
a Kenel of rachoes   a Skulke of theues
a Copill of spaynels   a Pontifical of prelates
a Sute of a typhin   a State of princes
a Caste of hawkes of   a Dignyte of chanons
  the tour .   a Trouthe of barons
a Caste of breed   Charge of curates
a Flight of goshaukes   a Lordship of monkes
a Flight of doutres   Supfluyte of nonnes
a Flight of cormerants   Prees of prestes
a Droue of nete   Scole of fysshe
a Tripe of gete   Scole of scolers
a Flock of shepe   Cluster of grapes
a Flock of lyse   Cluster of nottes
a Besynes of flyes   Cluster of carles
a Harepe of hors   Cluster of tame cattes
a Stode of mares   destruccyon of wilde cattes
a Ragge of coltes   Boste of souldyours
a Drifte of tame swyn   Threte of cortpars
a Sondre of wilde swyn   Laufters of hostelers
a Tripe of hares   Glosyng of tauerners

29. The list of collective nouns in the Cambridge copy of *The Horse, the Sheep and the Goose*. Cambridge, University Library, Oates 4061, leaf [b] 9 recto.

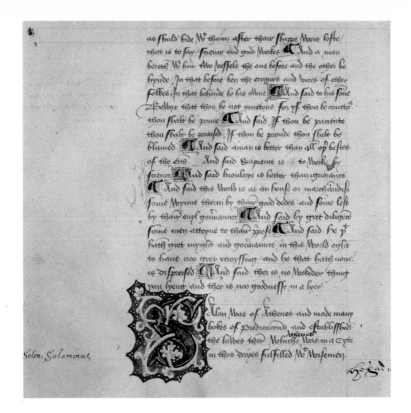

III. *The Dictes and Sayengs of the Philosophers*. A page of the manuscript completed for presentation to King Edward IV on 24 December 1477. Changes were inserted into the text after it had been copied from Caxton's first edition. Lambeth Palace Library, MS 265, leaf 17 verso.

IV. Offsets in the Malory manuscript. Printing ink over red and brown scribe's ink. British Library, MS Add. 59678, leaf 424 recto line 5.

v. Miniature portrait (enlarged detail) of Anthony Woodville, Earl Rivers, in the
Lambeth manuscript of the *Dictes*, 1477.
Lambeth Palace Library, MS 265, leaf 1 verso.

vi. Miniature portrait (enlarged detail) of Margaret of York, Duchess of Burgundy,
in a manuscript which she commissioned in Brussels – probably from the early
1470s.
British Library, MS Add. 7970, leaf 1 verso.

a Slouth of beres   a Trase of an hare
a Lees of grehoundes   a Skulke of foxes
a Brase of houndes   a Skulke of freres
a Kenel of racches   a Skulke of theues
a Copill of spanyels   a Pontifical of prelates
a Sute of a lyshm   a State of princes
a Caste of halbkes of the   a Dignite of chanons
   tour +   a Trouthe of barons
a Caste of breed   a Charge of curates
a Flight of goshalbkes   a Lordship of monkes
a Flight of douses   Supplupte of nonnes
a Flight of cormerants   Prees of prestes
a Droue of nete   Scole of fysshe
a Trippe of gete   Scole of scolers
a Flock of shepe   Cluster of grapes
a Flock of lyse   Cluster of nottes
a Besynes of flyes   Cluster of carles
a Hareys of hors   Cluster of tame cattes
a Stode of mares   destruction of Wilde cattes
a Raggh of coltes   Goste of souldyo· rs
a Drifte of tame swyn   Threte of coxtpar.
a Sondre of Wilde swyn   Labster of hostelers
   Trippe of hares   Glosyng of tauerners

30. The list of collective nouns in the copy at the Pierpont Morgan Library.
New York, Pierpont Morgan Library, PML 27473, leaf [b] 9 recto.

'a skulke of foxes' is extended to 'a skulke of freres' and of 'thieves'. And even more freely, there follows a procession of 'a State of princes', 'a Dignity of canons', 'a Lordship of Monks' and 'a Superfluity of nuns'.

In order to set his lists of nouns, the compositor had, of course, to use the indefinite article a at the beginning of each item. We see, however, that after 3½ columns, listing 77 nouns, the use of the article suddenly stopped at the same place in both editions. In the Cambridge book the compositor had used the round a in the lists and continued in the second column of one page suddenly with eight double *a*'s, twice skipping a line which should have started with 'a' (see Fig. 29). This in itself would be almost consistent with the preferences of the *Jason* compositor as we know them. He would have used the round *a* as long as he could, and only when he ran out of them, in dire necessity, he would have used the double *a*'s as a stop-gap measure. But he would have given up this attempt after ten lines, and also he would carefully have saved four round *a*'s to use in the middle of words (see Fig. 29, lines 1, 7, 21, 22 of column 2; the other *a*'s form part of ligatures).

However, when Paul Needham compared this page in the Cambridge book with the typesetting of the copy in the Pierpont Morgan Library (see Fig. 30) he came up with a far better explanation of what had happened in the Cambridge book, together with proof of the order of printing of the two editions. In the Morgan copy the lists are consistently set with double *a* at the beginning of the short lines. The double *a* has the function here of 'halfway' capital, and we recognise the style of the compositor of the first half of the *Canterbury Tales*. That the use of double *a*'s came to an end in the work of this compositor is much easier to explain than the behaviour of the compositor of the Cambridge book. The lists caused an unusually heavy run on double *a*'s, of which there were fewer than round *a*'s in the type case. At the point after the 'Lordship of Monks' the double *a*'s were used up. The compositor of the Morgan book then decided to use no *a* at all rather than to use the round *a* instead. He may have intended to add the double *a*'s later before tying up the page, as soon as some had come into circulation again, and then forgot about it.

It is clear that it cannot be coincidence that the use of *a*'s stopped at exactly the same place on the page in the Morgan and in the Cambridge books. One must have been copied from the other, and, as we can recognise the work of two different compositors by their different use of *a*, one used the work of the other as *exemplar*. The work of the compositor of the Morgan book seems to be a more consistent course of action (although we must allow him a lapse of memory) than what was done for the Cambridge book. As Paul Needham concluded, it is therefore far more likely that the Morgan book was the first and served as example for the book in Cambridge. The later book also offers a good example of another characteristic of the *Jason*-compositor', which we find especially in the quartos: he could easily be influenced by what he saw before him when he followed printed copy. In this particular instance he was more careless than his predecessor.

This, then, reverses the traditional order of two quarto editions. With similar but more complicated arguments set out by Dr Bühler it is possible to show the same for another of the quartos which was printed twice, *The Churl and the Bird*, while the order of the two *Cato* editions will also have to be reversed, since on the evidence of the paper used one belongs evidently to the earlier group. Of these two texts it is again the first edition that is in the USA, in the Pierpont Morgan Library, and in the Huntington Library in California, and the second edition that belongs to the group of quartos in Cambridge. The earlier group is generally set by the compositor of *Canterbury Tales* (first half) while the '*Jason* compositor' had an important hand in the second group of quartos.

NEW CHRONOLOGICAL ARRANGEMENT RESULTING FROM PAPER EVIDENCE

The evidence provided by paper leads in the first place to the distinction between an earlier and later group of quartos. This evidence can only be outlined here very briefly; it will be published in full by Paul Needham. The whole argument, both on typographical grounds and paper evidence, was first made public in 1980 in a BBC television programme with the title *The Printer's Tale*. Summarised, the paper evidence runs as follows:

Within the quarto-editions a distinction can now be made between an early group and a later group (to which the Cambridge quartos belong). The early group which comprises five or six books does not have any paper-stocks in common with any of the folio editions or later quartos. The later quartos, however, contain paper which is also found in the folios. The order in which the paper was used in the later quartos can only be interpreted in one way. Within this sequence of quartos, the earlier editions have paper in common with the *Canterbury Tales*, the later with *Jason* and *Dictes*, in that order. The order of first, *Jason* and then the *Dictes*, (which is the traditional one) is also confirmed by the fact that we find the same paper at the end of *Jason* and at the beginning of *Dictes*. The *Ordinale* found its place among the second group of quartos, as it has a paper-stock in common with the *Canterbury Tales*, while one copy of its advertisement is printed on paper with a watermark that is also found in *Jason* and *Dictes*.

The most important result of this new chronological arrangement is the new place here assigned to the *Canterbury Tales*. Caxton chose an English book with the widest possible appeal to begin his career in England. We shall return to this aspect later, but we shall first examine what the new find implied for Caxton's typography.

In the first place we must now rearrange the order of the list of Caxton's publications and his types on the basis of these findings:

	I EARLIEST GROUP	TYPE	
	Indulgence (before 13 Dec. 1476)	2	
	the word (I)Ohannes		3
5 quartos:	Lydgate, *The Horse, Sheep and Goose* I	2	
	Lydgate, *The Churl and the Bird* I	2	
	Lydgate, *Stans puer ad mensam*	2	
	Russell, *Propositio*	2	
	Cato I	2	
	Sarum Hours? (in-8°-or printed in Bruges)	2	
	II LATER GROUP A		
folio	Chaucer, *Canterbury Tales*	2	
concurrently:	Lydgate, *The Horse, Sheep and Goose* II	2	
5½ quartos	Lydgate, *The Churl and the Bird* II	2	
	Infantia Salvatoris	2	
	Lydgate, *Temple of glass*	2	
	Cato II (part)	2	
	Ordinale		3
	III LATER GROUP B		
folio	Lefèvre, *The History of Jason*	2 + 3	
('18 Nov. 1477'): folio	*The Dictes of the Philosophers*	2 + 3	
concurrently:	*Cato* II (part)	2	
3½ quartos	Chaucer, *Parlement of fowls*	2 + 3	
	Chaucer, *Anelida and Arcite*	2 + 3	
	Book of Courtesy	2 + 3	
	Advertisement for *Ordinale*		3
20 Feb. 1478	Chr. de Pisan, *Moral Proverbs*	2 + 3	
	Boethius, transl. Chaucer	2	3

68

The introduction of Caxton's Type 3

It is remarkable that in this sequence the books do really divide between books printed in Type 2 alone, and books printed in a combination of Type 2 with Type 3. The combinations occur only after Type 3 had been used for a full-scale book, the *Ordinale*. In fact, a distinction should also be made between books in which a deliberate, decorative use is made of the bold, emphatic character of Type 3, and books in which it seems to appear as a stop-gap measure. Type 3 was designed to be used in conjunction and deliberate contrast with Type 2 while it could also serve on its own for liturgical works. A similar combination was designed by Veldener almost immediately after Caxton's types and is seen in books printed in Bruges (Fig. 31), while he sometimes used Type 3

31. A combination of light and heavy type designed by Johannes Veldener: *Cato* in Latin and Dutch, printed at Bruges by Johannes Brito, *c.*1477, surviving only as a fragment.   Bruges, City Archive.

Abrotanū Aueronde

es heet inden ierſten droeg in
dē twedē A. teghḗt wytual
le des haers dat s alopiaa et
ſcorfeheyt of ſchellinghe des
hoets dat s tinea es auerond
ghelick alſen goet. den baert
of elders daer men gherne
haer hadde ſalmē ſtrikē met deſen om thaer of dē
baert haeſt te doen waſſen Nempt ſap van Auerode met dpl olp of olpe van ſquinati gheminge
teghen onſteltenis der borſt wye couder ſake ſiede
Auerode yſop caliſſibout in wat mz penye ʒuker

32. Caxton's Type 3 as used by Johannes Veldener in a Herbal, printed at Louvain in 1484. British Library, C.14.a.13(2), leaf 2 verso.

himself for headings in combination with a bastarda text type (Fig. 32). In Caxton's work this is how it is found in later books, for example, the *Boethius* where lines of Latin verse are printed in Type 3 which conveys a feeling of solid conclusiveness amid the airier lines of English prose in Type 2 (Fig. 33). In the earlier books,

33. Caxton's Type 2 and Type 3 used in deliberate contrast. Boethius, *De consolatione philosophiae* with the translation by Chaucer, printed by Caxton in 1478. British Library, IB.55018, leaf [i] 4 recto.

however, one finds only a sprinkling of Type 3 among the capitals, which can either be due to foul-case (i.e. errors in distributing type over the cases), or deliberate use of the type to eke out a short supply of certain letters. In *Jason* especially there are signs of shortage of type, probably because too much type was tied up in several books produced at the same time, a circumstance that is also suggested by the distribution of paper-stocks. We have seen that at the end of some pages the compositor of *Jason* ran out of round *a*'s and suddenly used exclusively the double *a*, a letter which he had hitherto in this book avoided altogether. Apparently he was also

71

short of the capital O of Type 2, for he sometimes used a filed Q for
O. But his use of the H of Type 3 had a different purpose. He used
it often for the name Hercules and for the exclamation Ha, as in 'Ha
Sir Knight', which is frequently encountered in this heroic text. Here
the heavier H from Type 3 was chosen for stylistic reasons, to put

re Amerous of polb as pe ke of her . And by thps loue
ske ke comen iŋ to this holbse after polb . Ha/a sir kmight
anslbezæ Jason, J haue no charge of that stroke, for my

Bekk Joyous for to knolbe him and thus saiæ to him by
ærysion .Ha/a right oultrageous folk/Arte thou ke that
arte affoyleð Bith the blanche feures for cause of my right

34. H of Type 3 used amid Type 2 for forceful exclamations by Jason.
British Library, C.10.b.3, leaves [f] 5 verso, [c] 2 recto.

extra emphasis on a breathy 'Ha!' (See Fig. 34). The occasional use
of Type 3 could clearly only be put into practice after the printing of
the *Ordinale*. Evidently it was by then fully available to Caxton and
put into circulation. But why only then?

Caxton's Type 3 is a type that was to become one of Johannes
Veldener's successes. Unlike Type 2, which was exclusive to Caxton
and for which Caxton may have owned the punches, Type 3 became
one of Veldener's more ambitious types. He sold it to printers in
Antwerp and Louvain (see Figs. 35 and 36) and used it himself to
good effect for headings in a Herbal (see Fig. 32). It is therefore

72

Libellus de Raptu anime Tundali
et eius visione Tractans de penis in
ferni et gaudijs paradisi·

Memēto preterita qlis fuerit tibi vita
Et que sunt merita tu morieris ita·

Ex libris F. Bruijninex·

35. Caxton's Type 3 used in Antwerp by Mathias van der Goes, c.1488.
British Library, IA.49918, title-page.

36. Caxton's Type 3 used in Louvain by Rudolphus Loeffs de Driel, *c*.1484.
The Hague, Royal Library, 169.G.33.

likely that the punches of this typeface remained with Veldener, but
Caxton must have owned a set of matrices, as we can infer from the
fact that we see the type used by other English printers. First a poor
casting of it was used by a partnership of two printers in London,
John Lettou and William de Machlinia. They squeezed the type into
the text-pages of their law-books set in a much smaller type, with the
result that the names of important speakers in legal cases jumped to
the eye. Type 3 was cast on a smaller body, and even then some
letters had to be filed down to achieve this effect (see Fig. 37).

37. Type 3 squeezed with difficulty into a page with much smaller text type.
Year-Book 33 Henry VI, London, John Lettou and William de Machlinia, *c*.1482.
British Library, IB.55422, leaf a 8 verso.

74

Another poor casting was used for headings in St. Albans by the Schoolmaster Printer (see Fig. 38). Much later an excellent new cast

Now ſhall þe knaw what theis terme
& moo folowyng . as Huf .Juttý ferrý
Raundon . Crepe . Ennewed .

38. Caxton's Type 3 in a poor casting used at St. Albans by the Schoolmaster Printer for *The Book of Hunting, Hawking and Blasing of Arms*.   British Library, G.10547, leaf d 1 recto.

was used by Caxton's successor Wynkyn de Worde who inherited his former master's typographical material. He used it in much the same way as Caxton had done himself in some of his books, to bold, declamatory effect (see Fig. 39). This new casting is in fact proof

Explicit libellus. quod Crede michi ap-
pellatur.perutilis Say cleris..ac perui-
gili opera correct9. & impreſſus in weſt-
monaſterio per wynkyn de worde. āno
domini.M).cccc.nonageſimoquinto.

Cuius ventilaby in manu eius.& pur-
gabit areā ſuā. Uerba hec quāuis euan-
gelica ſint .M)yſtice tamē & allegorice cō-
parari iſti libello poſſint ſic. vt predictū
eſt Ad laudē ventilatoris.ſic. Cuius in
māu vētilaby. id eſt.libellus iſte.purga-
bit areā ſuā .id eſt.glcientiaz i orando .

39. Type 3 was still in good shape when Wynkyn de Worde used a recasting for a colophon in 1495.   British Library, IA.55178, leaf C 8 recto.

that Caxton owned the matrices; it is therefore likely that he was generous and allowed his fellow printers in London and St. Albans to make use of a little of his material, admittedly in a not too successful version, and perhaps they even had to pay for the privilege.

On the evidence of the chronology of Caxton's early books one may deduce that after the high investment in Type 2, Caxton decided to go to even more expense and to purchase a set of matrices of Type 3, and this only after gaining some experience in Westminster. There is no trace of Type 3 in the *Canterbury Tales*, nor, more tellingly, in the small quartos produced concurrently, where there is no reason to expect typographical consistency. But what about the word (I)Ohannes in the Indulgence? (see Fig. 40). Is that not a

40. The word '[I]Ohannes' in the Indulgence, printed in Caxton's Type 3.   London, Public Record Office, Exchequer K. R. Ecclesiastical Documents 6/56 (detail). Cf. Fig. 11.

piece of irrefutable evidence that Type 3 existed early on in Caxton's career in England, and was in his hands?

Veldener is known to have tried out his types before producing them in a definitive version. We have seen such a trial of Caxton's Type 2, used by Veldener in one of his own books before it went to Caxton (Fig. 18). Perhaps we should risk, for once, a guess: was this word merely an experiment, a handful of letters given by the typefounder, whose name was Johannes, to persuade his customer that this new typeface on which he had just started to work would go well with the other type that he had recently delivered? 'Try this word,' he may have said, 'My name augurs well for a beginning.'

But before giving in entirely to such a flight of fancy we shall further consider Caxton's early books, and we may find in them another solution to the question posed by this isolated appearance of Type 3.

Dating the Dictes

There is one final blow to deal to the established chronology. The date 18 November 1477 for the completion of the *Dictes* was known since Ames and confirmed by Blades. Blades looked at the book with a printer's eye and decided that in the one copy containing this date, the whole page on which the additional colophon is found after the end of the text was printed at one single pull (see Colour plate I).

The *Dictes* offers a complicated textual problem, which was studied at great length by Dr C. F. Bühler. Caxton printed a second edition of the *Dictes* with considerable revision, and strangely enough, this edition bears a colophon with the same date, 18 November 1477, although the book is printed in the second state of Type 2, used not earlier than late 1478 or 1479; moreover on paper evidence we can be quite certain that it was printed in 1480. Here then we have a witness who surely is lying. However, the other witness, i.e. Caxton's first edition, is not beyond suspicion. Apart from the two Caxton editions of the *Dictes* there is a manuscript of Earl Rivers' translation now in Lambeth Palace Library, which was completed for presentation to King Edward IV on 24 December 1477. It has a well-known miniature showing the presentation of the manuscript by Earl Rivers and its scribe to the King and his court, including the Queen and the young Prince of Wales for whose perusal the translation was in the first place intended (see Colour plate V). With its elaborate initials and spacious layout it shows up Caxton's printed book as a second-rate product, not fit to be owned by a king (see Colour plate III). The manuscript was demonstrably copied from a copy of Caxton's first edition of the *Dictes*, but contains many of the textual features of the second edition which were partly inserted as discreet corrections. How was it possible to copy, to correct extensively and decorate lavishly a substantial manuscript between the date of completion of the printed book, 18 November, and 24 December, a period which can be calculated to have contained only about 27 working days?

The answer was found on renewed examination of the copy of the *Dictes* in the John Rylands Library in Manchester. One hesitates to differ in opinion from a typographer as experienced as Blades. However, under oblique light it was not too difficult to establish that on the last page the end of the text was printed first (causing indentations on the other side of the leaf); that these were flattened by the impression of the penultimate page, (which caused relief on the page first printed), but that the colophon was printed last of all, causing new markings on the page that had first been flattened. In other words, Caxton's press printed the outer forme first, the inner forme last, and the colophon was added later.

The wording of the added colophon is 'Thus endeth this book of the dyctes and notable wyse sayenges of the phylosophers late translated and drawen out of frenshe into our englisshe tonge by my forsaide lord Therle of Ryvers and lord Skales .and by hys comandement sette in forme and emprynted in this manere as ye maye here in this booke see Whiche was fynisshed the .xviij. day of the moneth of Novembre. the sevententh yere of the regne of kyng Edward the fourth'. 'This book' signified therefore in this case 'this copy of a book', 'this copy with a colophon added later', or 'the object in your hands', and not the whole edition. The colophon of the Lambeth manuscript, written not much later, has almost identical wording (see Fig. 41). When applied to a manuscript the word 'book' must

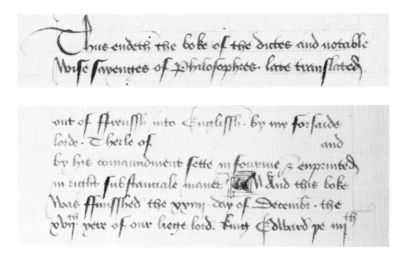

41. The colophon in the Lambeth manuscript of the *Dictes*. Lambeth Palace Library, MS 265, leaf 105 verso, leaf 106 recto (details).

of course always have the meaning of 'the book in your hands', exactly the same meaning, therefore, as in the added printed colophon of the *Dictes*.

In conclusion the date of 18 November 1477 vanishes as the date for the whole edition of the *Dictes*, and also as a date to which particular significance has to be attached as documenting the earliest printing in England. The dating '1477' stands, for Caxton began his epilogue to the work with the words 'enprynted . . . . . at Westmestre the yere of our Lord .M.CCCC.Lxxvij.' (see Fig. 42). This

78

Ere endeth the book named the dictes or sayengis of the philosophhres enprynted, by me William Caxton at Westmestre the yere of our lord ✠M✠ CCCC✠ lxxvij✠ Whiche book is late translated out of Frensshe into englysshe ✠ by the Noble and puissant lord, Lord Antone Erle of Ryuyers lord of Scales & of the Ile of Wyght, Defendour and directour of the siege apostolique, for our holy Fader the Pope in this Royame of Englond and Gouernour of my lord Prynce of Wales And It is so that at suche tyme as he had accomplysshid this sayd Werke, it liked him to sende it to me in certayn quayers to ouersee, Whiche forthwith I sawe & fonde therin many grete, notable, and wyse sayengis of the philosophres Accordyng vnto the bookes made in frensshe Whiche I had ofte afore redd, But certaynly I had seen none in englissh til that tyme, And so afterward I cam vnto my sayd lord & told him how I had red & seen his book, And that he had don a meritory dede in the labour of the translacion therof in to our englissh tunge, Wherin he had deseruid a singuler laude & thank &c, Thenne my sayd lord desired me to ouersee it and where as I sholde fynde faute to correcte it, Wherein I answerd vnto his lordship, that I coude not amende it, But if I sholde so presume I might apaire it, For it was right wel & connyngly made & translated into right good and fayr englissh, Notwithstondyng he willed me to ouersee it & shewid me dyuerse thinges Whiche as him semed myght be left out as diuerse lettres missiues sent from Alisander to dari9 and aristotle & eche to other, Whiche lettres were lityl appertinent vnto to dictes

42. The beginning of Caxton's epilogue to the *Dictes* with the date 1477.
British Library, IB.55005, leaf [k] 2 recto.

allows the scribe of the Lambeth manuscript an unspecified length of time in the year 1477 (which could either have been reckoned from 1 January or from 25 March) for copying, correcting and decorating the text in manuscript.

THE DATE OF THE INTRODUCTION OF PRINTING INTO ENGLAND RECONSIDERED

As for dating the beginning of Caxton's career in England, the disappearance of the date in November 1477 is no longer a severe disappointment. The chronological sequence of Caxton's early books in Westminster remains intact. It has acquired a much firmer basis than before, since paper and use of types as witnesses of what happened in the printing house corroborate each other's evidence. We find further corroboration in the Westminster leases which, as Howard Nixon has shown, do not indicate the date when Caxton first settled in Westminster.

Until early September 1475 Caxton was very busily engaged in the Low Countries. It was, as Painter called it, his 'finest hour' in the service of the King who entrusted him with the task of chartering a fleet by hiring ships in Dutch cities. Caxton's movements in both the northern and the southern Netherlands are recorded in a variety of documents, ranging from safe-conducts to the record of his mediation in a dispute concerning a ship that had stranded on one of the treacherous sandbanks in the shallows of Zeeland. Especially from 1460 on, when his official status had risen, these records recur frequently. In the last thirteen months of Caxton's official activities we know of the following commitments:

10 August 1474	Witness to ratification of treaty between Edward IV and Hansa, at the Carmelite monastery in Bruges
November 1474	Caxton is described as resident in Flanders in a plea in Chancery brought by his fellow mercer John Neve
1 December 1474	Caxton commissioned by the King to treat in delegation with commissaries of the Duke of Burgundy
28 January 1975	Plea in Chancery endorsed
20 April 1475	A letter concerning the relations between the Hansa and the King shows that Caxton was resident in Bruges and was concerned with relations with the Hansa settlement in Bruges

80

23 April–June 1475	Tour of Holland to hire a fleet from Dutch cities with official support; included are Delft, Rotterdam, Gouda, Dordrecht, Zierikzee, Goes, Reimerswaal, Middelburg and Vlissingen
27 May	Visits the northern cities of Hoorn and Enkhuizen
June	Officially received by the City of Gouda
early July 1475(?)	Attended at St-Omer a meeting between Edward IV, Margaret of York, Gloucester and Clarence (?)
20 August 1475	Royal warrant from Westminster to witness final exchange of ratification documents between Edward IV and Hansa
4 September 1475	Caxton is witness of final ratification of treaty between Edward IV and Hansa at the Augustinian monastery in Bruges

A full agenda, by all accounts. From September 1475 on there is on the contrary not a single record to witness Caxton's presence in the Low Countries.

The chronological sequence of the printing of Caxton's early books in Westminster now begins therefore at an undetermined date, which could be early in 1476 or possibly even late 1475. Caxton started with a few small books, working with one small press. He then began to print the *Canterbury Tales*, the first Westminster book in folio, while also continuing the production of small quartos. Perhaps the *Canterbury Tales* was printed on two presses working concurrently, and, as we have seen, there were at least two compositors at work by that time. The Indulgence was printed while this was in progress, in 1476, at any time between 24 May, when Abbot John Sant (whose name is printed at the beginning of the document) was appointed as papal nuncio and commissary for the sale of this Indulgence, and 13 December, when the one surviving copy was issued. There now remains no reason whatever to assign the Indulgence to an early place in Caxton's production. On the contrary, if we assume that it was printed shortly before 13 December, Type 3 was probably in use for the *Ordinale*, which was set from a complete typecase, and the word 'Johannes' in the Indulgence takes its place with the other early appearances of Type 3. The *History of Jason* was printed after the *Canterbury Tales*, and it is likely that by this time we have reached 1477; the *Dictes* was, according to Caxton's own epilogue printed in 1477, and must have been completed before 18 November of that year, the date of the colophon added to one surviving copy, and probably one or two more, no longer extant. The date for the very small *Moral Proverbs* is 20 February 1478, and the completion of the *Boethius*, which has paper-stocks in common with it, will have been later, or perhaps even a little earlier. We then have no printed date for any Caxton books until 24 March 1479, when he completed printing of the translation into English by Earl Rivers of the *Cordiale*. This was preceded (as paper evidence shows) by only one undated book, the *Nova Rhetorica*, in which, as in the *Cordiale*, renewed typographical material appears in the form of a new casting of Type 2. There seems therefore to have been an interval in Caxton's activities as publisher and printer during most of 1478, which followed a period of sustained activity in 1476 and 1477.

It is not possible to estimate the minimum period of time required for producing this output, as we have done with the Bruges books. The early quartos, the *Canterbury Tales*, the quartos produced concurrently and the *Ordinale* add up to about 273 edition sheets (or about 293 if one includes the first edition of the *Sarum Hours*). *Jason*, *Dictes* and the last group of quartos add up to 128 edition sheets. While allowing for a date of introduction of printing in Westminster well before September 1476, these figures do not help us as an indication of the date by which Caxton must have started production, due to the more complicated organization of his workshop.

The chronology of Caxton's early books at which we now have arrived can be summarized briefly in a final table:

BRUGES

I
undated
(late 1473 / early 1474)   *Recuyell*
31 March 1474   *Chess* I

II
undated
(between 31 March 1474   4 later Bruges folios, in French
and summer 1475)   *Sarum Hours* ? (or Westminster)

WESTMINSTER

I
undated   5 quartos
                                 Sarum Hours ? (or Bruges)

II
undated
(1476)   *Canterbury Tales* concur-   5½ quartos
                                              rently :
                                        (between 24 May
                                          and 13 Dec. 76):   *Indulgence*
                                                              Ordinale

III
undated
(early 1477 ?)   *Jason*   concur-   3½ quartos
                                                  rently :   Advertise-
                                                             ment for
                                                             Ordinale

1477, before 18 Nov.   *Dictes*
20 Feb. 1478   *Moral Proverbs*
undated
(early 1478)   *Boethius*

Further investigation of Caxton's books: his patrons

So far we have used the results of the material investigation for only one purpose, to establish a chronology of Caxton's books. The priority given to this question hardly needs an explanation: in any attempt to get closer to the truth it is of the first importance to arrange events in the right order, in this case the order in which editions left the press. However, while doing so the evidence provided us also with some insight into Caxton's rapidly expanding printing business. At first this consisted of one press, with one compositor working for it, using one typeface; soon one, possibly even two larger presses were added (working concurrently on the two halves of the *Canterbury Tales*); another compositor can be recognized; and another typeface made its appearance. It has even been possible to have a quite close look at the compositors as they were at work.

But there is more to this kind of investigation, and this proves to have direct bearing on the circumstances of the production of Caxton's early books. This concerns his early publishing programme and his patrons. In the first place it is remarkable that after Caxton's printing career in Bruges where he had sought the patronage of Margaret of York and of the Duke of Clarence, he set out in Westminster to all appearances with no patronage at all. *The Canterbury Tales*, which we now know was the first major book printed in Westminster, was published, as far as we can tell, as an independent venture, and the small quartos show no sign either of having been printed to order or under special protection. It is only in 1477 that the printing of the *Dictes* was commissioned by its translator, Anthony Woodville, Earl Rivers, who subsequently can be linked with several of Caxton's publications. *The History of Jason* which preceded the *Dictes* and was dedicated by Caxton to the Prince of Wales 'under the protection and suffrance . . . of the king' may also have had the backing of Earl Rivers.

EARL RIVERS AND THE *DICTES*

The textual relationship between the printed editions of the *Dictes* and the Lambeth manuscript, which has now become clearer, can tell us something of Caxton's relationship to this patron. Anthony Woodville, Earl Rivers (see Colour plate v) was a brother of the Queen and closely connected with the court. He represented the

King on many occasions, and was given a position of special confidence when he was appointed as Governor to the Prince of Wales in 1473. Among the instructions for the Prince's education issued by the King was the express wish that 'such noble stories as behoves a prince to understand' should be read to him. This suited the taste of Earl Rivers, who, besides a gallant knight and, as we shall see, a profoundly devout man, was without doubt the figure in the royal entourage most inclined to *belles lettres*. He may have owned a number of fine manuscripts, two of which have come down to us, one with his own signature (see Fig. 43) and one with that of his widow Marie Rivers.

43. Signature of Earl Rivers ('Arivieres') with his motto in a manuscript of a collection of works of Christine de Pisan. It is written next to those of his mother Jacquetta of Luxembourg, and of Louis, Seigneur de Gruuthuse, the Bruges nobleman to whom he may have presented the manuscript.
British Library, MS Harl. 4431, fly-leaf.

Earl Rivers' deep devotion appears from the pilgrimages he had undertaken to Santiago de Compostella and to Rome, where he had become personally acquainted with that most literary-minded pope, Sixtus IV. He was even described by Caxton as 'defensor and director of the causes apostolique for our holy fader the Pope in this Royaume of England'. It is necessary to bear all this in mind when we look again at the *Dictes*.

In the long epilogue which Caxton added to the *Dictes* he explains that Rivers had asked him to 'oversee' (to read critically) his translation before printing it, and to correct it where required. Caxton had protested that he was in no way capable of improving what his lordship had written, but Rivers had insisted. Therefore Caxton had amended the text, and had noticed that Rivers had omitted certain passages, in which Socrates made disparaging remarks about women. Caxton humorously elaborated reasons for Rivers to play safe and stay in the good books of the ladies; his patron was, after all, at that time the most eligible widower in England. Caxton then added the omitted passages, for, like any conscientious merchant, he had a mild obsession about completeness and delivering all the goods. He gave the date of printing only at the beginning of his long piece of prose which occupies six pages (see Fig. 42). There are signs, however, that the noble earl was not pleased with the effects of Caxton's interference. The second edition incorporates many textual corrections; some of these derive from an earlier translation into English which had come to the translator's notice only recently, but many are independent. We have seen that part of the textual corrections found in the second printed edition are first found in the Lambeth manuscript. We have also seen that the colophon of the Lambeth manuscript has words that are very close to those of the printed colophon added on 18 November 1477. The three versions, *Dictes* I – 1477, *Dictes* I – 18 November 1477 and Lambeth manuscript, 24 December 1477, therefore represent successive stages in the development of the text which terminated in the final version, fully corrected, which was printed in 1480 but bears the date 18 November 1477. It is as if Caxton made amends to his patron, who only now, in 1480, received the book in the form it should have had on some unspecified date before 18 November 1477.

OTHER BOOKS CONNECTED WITH EARL RIVERS

There may have been bitter words in between. We can only hear Caxton's side of the exchange. He seems to protest a good deal. The next book connected with Rivers is *The Moral Proverbs*. It is a delightful book, of only a few leaves, with a translation by Earl Rivers of some of Christine de Pisan's moral observations in verse. One of the surviving manuscripts once owned by Earl Rivers contains this text in French. The translation into English was printed by Caxton a few months after the incident of the *Dictes* colophon, and after the completion of the manuscript copy of the *Dictes*, in February 1478. In the colophon, added by Caxton in his own verse, he found it necessary to state that he did not change *one* word in the author's manuscript, that he calls the earl's secretary as witness to the truth of this statement, and he gave the date twice, once in verse and once in an additional line below the colophon: 'In February the cold season' (see Fig. 44). 'Master William', the earl must have said, among other remarks, 'a booklover *always* dates his books', or words to that effect.

Go thou litil quayer, and recomaunde me
Vnto the goode grace, of my special lorde
Therle Ryuers. for I haue enprinted the
At his comandement. folowyng euery worde
His coppe, as his secretaire can recorde
At Westmestre. of feuerer the .xx. daye
And of kyng Edward / the .xvij. yere lraye

Enprinted by Caxton
In feuerer the colde seasoy

44. Caxton's own verse at the end of Earl Rivers' translation of the *Moral Proverbs* of Christine de Pisan. Reproduced from the facsimile edition by William Blades, London 1859.

The next time Caxton printed a work by Earl Rivers was in the following year. It is the translation of the *Cordiale*. Here Caxton is also extremely explicit about dates: he states that he received the author's manuscript on the day of the Purification of the blessed Lady, falling on Tuesday 2 February, and that he finished printing on the day before the Annunciation of Our Lady, that is on 24 March. This has always been read as a boast of Caxton that he printed the book in a very short time. But let us look at the calendar

lastyng permanence in heuen Amen . Whiche werke present I begañ the morñ after the saide Purificacionof our blissid Lady. Whiche was the the daye of Seint Blase Bisshop and Martir . And finisshed on the euen of thannunciacion of our said blissid Lady fallyng on the wednesday the xxiiij daye of Marche . In the xix yere of kyng Edwarde the fourthe

45. Caxton's colophon to Earl Rivers' translation of the *Cordiale*. The mention of the weekday and the regnal year determine that the year was 1479 (i.e. 1478 based on the Lady Day year style). British Library, C.11.c.2, leaf [k] 5 verso.

	d	Sancte Brigide Jgnaci epi et pfessor.
ri	e	Purificacio beate Marie
rir	f	Sancti Blasi
viii	g	Sancti Gilberti
	A	Sancte Agathe
rvi	b	Scōr Hedasti et Amādi et Dorothee
v	c	Sancti Anguli episcopi
	d	Scōr pauli epi Luci et Ciriaci
riii	e	Sancte Appollonie
ii	f	Sancte Scolastice
	g	Sancte B ̄ lie virginis
r	A	Sce Eulalie virginis Sol in pisce
	b	Sancti wulstranni
rviii	c	Sancti Valentini
vii	d	faustini et Joniti
	e	Sancte Juliane virginis
rv	f	Sancti policronii episcopi et martiris
iiii	g	Sancti Symeonis epi et martiris
	A	Sabini Juliani Marcelli
rii	b	Sancte Mildrede virginis
i	c	
	d	Cathedra sancti petri
ir	e	policarpi Locus bisexti.
	f	Sancti Mathie apostoli
rvii	g	Jnuencio sancti pauli apostoli Rome
vi	A	Scōr martirū fortunati cū rr septem
	b	Sancti Augustini
riiii	c	Sancti Oswaldi episcopi et pfessoris

iii	d	Sancti Dauid episcopi
	e	Sancti Cedde episcopi
ri	f	Sanctorum Maurini et Alberti
	g	Sancti Adriani
rir	A	Scōr fore Eulchii perpetue et fe.
viii	b	Sanctoru Victoris et Victorini
	c	perpetue et felicitatis
rvi	d	Depolicio sancti felicis epi et pfesso.
v	e	Quadraginta martirum
	f	Sancte Agape virginis
riii	g	Sanctor Quirion et Candidi
ii	A	Sancti Gregorii pape
	b	Sancte Theodore martiris
r	c	petri martiris Sol in Ariete Equoc.
	d	Sancti Longini martiris
rviii	e	Scōr martirū Hillarii et Tacoam
vii	f	Sci patrici epi Geretrudis vginis
	g	Sancti Edwardi regis
rv	A	Sancti Joseph sponse beate marie v.
iiii	b	Sancti ... alberti
	c	Sancti Benedicti
rii	d	Sancti Affrodosii episcopi
i	e	Sancti Theodori presbiteri
	f	Sancti Agapiti martiris
ir	g	Annunciacio dominica
	A	Sancti Cr ... ris martiris
rvii	b	Resurrectio domini principale
vi	c	Sancte Dorothee virginis
	d	Sancti Victorini
riiii	e	Sancti Quirini
iii	f	Sancti Adelini episcopi

A ii

46. A calendar according to Sarum usage, printed by Wynkyn de Worde c.1494. Shown are the months of February and March. The feast days of obligation are printed in red and begin with a lombard initial (with the exception of the Annunciation).   British Library, C.21.c.20 (1), leaves A 1 verso, A 2 recto.

in use in the diocese of Canterbury at that time (see Fig. 46). One can calculate that between Wednesday 2 February and Wednesday 24 March 1479 there were seven Sundays and four feast days of obligation (Cathedra Petri on 22 February, St. Matthew on 24 February which coincided that year with Ash Wednesday, St. Gregory on 12 March and St. Edward on 18 March). On these days a printing house would not have been allowed to work. This leaves 39 working days. The book contains 38 printed sheets. One sheet per day is exactly the rate the sources (scant though they are) on printing house production in the fifteenth and sixteenth century indicate as the normal output for one press. Efficient, yes, but nothing to boast about at length. But in a context of gentle dispute about the function of colophons and the convention of dating, Caxton's statement may reveal the intention of giving exact, absolutely *exact*, dating, if that was what his patron seemed to require. It should also be noted that the two feasts between which printing took place were both feast days for the Holy Virgin; Lady Day (25 March) was the date of the

88

beginning of the ecclesiastical year and 24 March was therefore a traditional day for completing a commitment or a contract. But more significantly, the explicit mention of the two feast days must lead to the observation that Earl Rivers, who had a special devotion to the Virigin Mary, had reasons other than amorous for not wishing to deprecate women.

The *Cordiale* is the last publication in which Earl Rivers was explicitly mentioned. On the record of these three publications alone (*Dictes, Moral Proverbs* and *Cordiale*) he was undoubtedly Caxton's most influential patron. His influence may even have extended further. First there is the question, which so far cannot be raised beyond mere speculation, whether Rivers had anything to do with Caxton's printing of the *Officium visitationis beatae Mariae Virginis*. Pope Sixtus IV had promulgated a new form of this service for a feast day for Our Lady in 1475. This was the form printed by Caxton in 1480 (a date established with certainty from paper evidence). Only in 1481 the Convocation of Canterbury petitioned the Archbishop to order the feast in his province. Caxton's edition therefore anticipated this event, and may be seen as a piece of propaganda for the introduction of the feast, or for this particular devotion. Earl Rivers was described by Caxton in the *Dictes* and in the *Cordiale* as 'defensor and director of the causes apostolique for our holy fader the Pope.' On a pilgrimage to Rome Rivers had obtained an indulgence from Pope Sixtus IV for the chapel of St. Mary the Virgin in the Church of St. Stephen in the palace of Westminster, and he was described as having a singular devotion to this chapel. However, these circumstances together, and the fact that he was a devout man, although suggestive, are yet not sufficient grounds for assigning the initiative for this edition to him.

EARL RIVERS AND CAXTON'S EDITION OF *LE MORTE DARTHUR*

Finally we must turn to a much more ambitious publication of Caxton, Thomas Malory's *Le Morte Darthur*. This voluminous book was completed by Caxton on 31 July 1485, well after Earl Rivers had been executed in Pontefract Castle on 26 June 1483. The trails pointing to Earl Rivers as the instigator of the printing of this book have recently become much clearer, although Caxton had gone to considerable length to blur them.

In the prologue to the printed *Morte Darthur*, which together with the *Canterbury Tales* is Caxton's most lasting contribution to English literature, Caxton refers with studied vagueness to 'a certain

89

gentleman' who delivered the manuscript for the book to him. Recently it has become possible to identify the manuscript, and probably also the gentleman. The manuscript is the 'Winchester Manuscript', long preserved in Winchester College, which was acquired by the British Library in 1976, and has been called 'Malory Manuscript' since. It has on various blank pages scribbles and names which were studied by Hilton Kelliher after the manuscript had arrived in its new home. One such name in particular, Richard Followell, can be shown to be connected with the Malory family, and it seems likely that during the sixteenth century the manuscript was in the hands of that family, and near relations.

There are, however, also signs that it had not continuously remained with the family of its author. Ever since its discovery in Winchester in 1934 the manuscript had been considered an independent source for Malory's text, as it differs in many places from the text as printed in Caxton's edition. But there are traces that could indicate that the manuscript had been in Caxton's printing house: a fragment of an indulgence printed by Caxton was used to repair a leaf; and more intriguingly, there were smudges of printing ink, and some very faint offsets of printing types which only Caxton possessed. As any direct connexion between Caxton and the manuscript conflicted with the generally accepted textual arguments about the relation of the two sources, it was necessary to make a very careful investigation of the faint traces of Caxton's types.

The story of this research has been partly told in 1977 in an article in the British Library Journal. In short, it was necessary to differentiate between the shapes caused by offsets and all the other accidental smudges and stains that can be found in a well used manuscript. Offsets are caused by letters printed with printing ink which is oil-based, and which is therefore an essentially different substance from scribe's ink which is water-based. The main purpose of the investigation was therefore to show by optical means the difference between the two substances (and between them and any dirt or other undefinable matter). Once the investigator's eye (mine) was aware of the different shades of ink, the observations were not too difficult, especially as by then I was thoroughly familiar with the shapes of Caxton's printing types. In the end the shapes could be detected with the naked eye, sometimes even on the sensitive facsimile-edition of the manuscript. However, the difficulty lay in presenting the evidence to others. Once again, the courtroom comes to mind as a comparable situation. It was necessary to convince a jury, which in this case consisted of sceptical textual historians. The process of making the ghosts of Caxton's types visible to others developed slowly, step by step, as increasingly sophisticated aids became available. The difference between scribe's ink and printer's ink had shown up beautifully under a hand-held infra-red viewer, but unfortunately infra-red photography had fallen short of these results. A few years later the British Library acquired a Video Spectral Comparator with a wide range of filters and a short-circuit television display screen from which photographs can be taken. Now the earlier observations were fully borne out, and photographs taken from the screen were an improvement on earlier photography (see

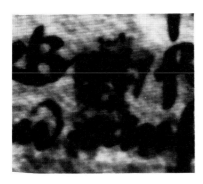

47. Offsets of two capitals of Caxton types in the Malory manuscript; photographs taken from the screen of the Video Spectral Comparator using infra-red filter. Left: capital I of Type 2. Right: capital F of Type 4. British Library, MS Add.59678, leaves 187 verso, line 6; 159 recto, line 13.

Fig. 47). Yet there was some loss of definition of the faint typographical shapes. In the end, after script, smudges and typography had been distinguished beyond doubt, colour photography through a binocular microscope using low magnification gave yet another image which showed both the contrast in texture and colour of the two kinds of ink (see Colour plate IV). A reading from the Visualtek screen, reversing the image, clearly showed Caxton's type (see Fig. 48).

But the material evidence is only the beginning of a complex textual argument. As in the Vatican manuscript of the *Nova Rhetorica* used as printer's copy by Caxton's compositors, we have here an example that brings us close to what actually happened with a text under the hands of Caxton's workmen. However, with the *Morte Darthur* the relationship is not as immediate as between printer's copy and printed text. The Malory manuscript had not been in the hands of Caxton's compositors: there are none of the signs of casting off made by compositors that we have learned to recognise. Yet the material evidence had shown that it had been near enough to Caxton's workshop, for offsets are most likely to have been caused by

91

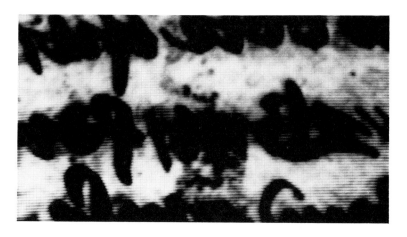

48. A reversed image of the offset of capital I of Type 2; photograph
taken from the Visualtek screen.   British Library, MS Add. 59678,
leaf 187 verso, line 6.

freshly printed sheets still damp with printer's ink. We must assume,
then, that someone (either Caxton or another person) used the
Malory manuscript that he had borrowed in order to prepare a
revised version in manuscript; subsequently this was marked up for
the compositors and used by them. This intermediate stage would
now be lost. Many of the differences between the Malory manuscript
and Caxton's text would have been introduced deliberately when the
text was edited for printing in this way. The most conspicuous is the
division of the text into chapters which made the text much more
manageable. It was pointed out by Caxton in his prologue, as a
recommendation for his edition. While copying and editing the text
slight improvements (to the copier's mind) were constantly introduced. Variations were made both voluntarily and by accident. The
next phase, however, setting the text in type with the intermediate
manuscript phase as *exemplar*, left also its mark on the text.
Compositors would invent their own corrections and improvements, and would introduce their own mistakes.

Sometimes an obvious error in the production of a book can bring
us closer to understanding what happened in the various phases. For
example, in one instance in the printed book some words are
repeated and are found both at the end of a page and at the
beginning of the next one. Caxton's text reads:

92

of this twelue moneth/ And Morgan le fay kynge Vrpens
wyf sente it me yester daye by a dwerf to this entent that I
shold slee kynge Arthur her broder/ For ye shall vnderstand

entente to slee kyng Arthur her broder/ for ye shal vnderstand
kynge Arthur is the man in the world that she moost hateth
by cause she is moost of worship and of prowesse of ony of her

49. Thomas Malory, *Le Morte Darthur*. The end of page g 1 verso and the
beginning of page g 2 recto in Caxton's edition. From the facsimile edition, edited by
Paul Needham, London 1976.   By courtesy of Scolar Press.

[g 1 verso] . . . entente that I // shold slee kynge Arthur her
broder / For ye shall vnderstand [g 2 recto] entente to slee kyng
Arthur her broder / for ye shal vnderstand . . .

The Malory manuscript reads here (in the middle of a page):

. . . entente to sle kynge Arthure hir brothir for ye shall vndir-
stonde y^t kynge Arthur ys the man . . .

50. The same passage in the Malory manuscript.   British Library, MS Add. 59678,
leaf 54 recto.

We may be able to understand what went wrong here when we
realize that in cast-off copy the line where a new page should begin
would be indicated by a stroke, sometimes two strokes, or a cross. In
this case it must have been difficult for the compositor to decide
which line was indicated. When he began setting page g 2 recto the
compositor thought it was the line beginning with *entente*. Page g 1
verso probably had to be completed after page g 2 recto had been
set and printed. The compositor had to invent some extra words and
longer forms to fill up space. We can see how he made his line longer
by printing Caxton's text in this way:

g 1^v, last lines: entente that I // shold   slee kynge Arthur her
g 2^r, first line: entente   to slee kyng   Arthur her

g 1^v: broder / For ye shall vnderstand //
g 2^r: broder / for ye shal vnderstand //

On g 1 verso he managed to expand the length of his line by adding 10 letters and introducing the use of a capital. It was evidently necessary to end the pages *exactly* as cast off, and yet to make it look like a page filled to normal length, a 'seamless' transition to the following page. When the compositor ended page g 1 verso he thought that the stroke in his exemplar indicated the line *following* the one beginning with *entente* as the spot where g 2 recto had started – wishful thinking, no doubt, as he had obviously too much space on his hands. This is therefore what the exemplar must have looked like:

... kyng Vryence wyf sente it me yesterday by a dwarf to this
× entente to slee kyng Arthur her broder / for ye shall vnderstand
that kyng Arthur is the man in the world that she most hateth ...

In this slow, tortuous manner we are brought nearer to what happened to a manuscript once it was in the hands of the printer. Here the investigation helps us to visualise the direct derivation of the printed text from the Malory manuscript, via the intermediate copy. It can also help to bring us closer to the patron who procured the manuscript. When Kelliher had established that the manuscript could through the name of Richard Followell be linked with the Malory family of Litchborough in Northamptonshire in the sixteenth century, he also noted that the Woodville family had close ties with this county, and that in fact they derived from Grafton, a village only ten miles from Litchborough, of which they still held a lordship in the time of Anthony Woodville Earl Rivers. Now that the connexion between Caxton's edition and the Malory manuscript seems well established, it appears certainly within the bounds of possibility that it was on Earl Rivers' initiative that Caxton started to prepare the book for printing. Kelliher pointed out that this may again have been in the Earl's capacity as Governor of the Prince of Wales in order to provide suitably instructive reading material. Two years after Rivers' execution in 1483, when Caxton completed printing the book, at the time when the reign of Richard III had not quite come to an end, it would still have been impossible for him to refer openly to his patronage in the prologue.

The offsets of Caxton types, the intricate textual argument and the investigation of the ties between the two families are all tenuous traces which do, however, all seem to point in one direction – that Caxton's 'certain gentleman' was none other than Earl Rivers, the patron of his early years in Westminster and the enthusiastic supporter of the art of printing in England.

The fate of royal patrons was particularly uncertain. Of Caxton's four early patrons Earl Rivers, the Prince of Wales and the Duke of Clarence all died as victims of political violence. Caxton's first patroness, Margaret of York, Duchess of Burgundy and sister of Edward IV, also suffered at the hand of political fortune.

Apart from the printing of *The Recuyell of the Histories of Troye* the duchess Margaret also commissioned sequences of manuscripts from famous scribes in Brussels and Ghent (see Colour plate VI). One wonders if she may have commissioned more printed books from Caxton than have come to the surface. Among the books printed in Bruges the *Méditations sur les psaumes pénitentiaux* and the first *Cordiale* (in French), as well as the beautiful *Sarum Hours* (bibliographers find it impossible to decide whether it should remain assigned to the press in Westminster, or be ceded to Bruges) – these books would all fit in remarkably well with the splendid manuscripts containing devotional texts the Duchess is known to have commissioned and owned. In any case, her power, as a patron and otherwise, came to an abrupt end early in 1477 when her spouse Charles the Bold was killed in battle before Nancy in his campaign against the Swiss and their allies. From then on she is not known to have commissioned any manuscripts or printed books.

Careful scrutiny of another of Caxton's early Westminster books reveals an abrupt change of course which may reflect these (or else similar) misfortunes. It is *The History of Jason*, printed between the *Canterbury Tales* and the *Dictes* of 1477, and therefore probably completed some time early in 1477.

The book as issued was dedicated to Edward, Prince of Wales, then six years old, and it may again not be too fanciful to recognise Rivers' influence here. But there are signs that the Prince of Wales is not the dedicatee originally intended by Caxton. Dr. C. F. Bühler noticed in one of his many studies of variations between copies of Caxton editions that two sheets in the first quire of the book exist in two settings. That is, the outer formes are known only in one single setting, but the inner formes (four pages altogether) each exist in two different settings (see Fig. 51). This indicates a division of work in the printing house: a division over two presses, in order to speed up the completion of these two sheets.

The first leaves of *Jason* may reveal more about Caxton's intentions, if we look carefully at the last vestiges of evidence that has otherwise vanished. The two sheets which exist in two settings are printed on paper that is found nowhere else in the book or in Caxton's printing. The other sheets in the first quire form a continuous sequence with what follows in the book. This in itself does not prove anything, but should arouse our suspicions: printed

51. The setting of the first quire of *The History of Jason*.

Compositor I is the '*Canterbury Tales* compositor'; Compositor II is the '*Jason* compositor'.

1 recto: p.1 blank	8 verso: p.16 TEXT Compositor I	outer sheet, not replaced
1 verso: p.2 blank	8 recto: p.15 TEXT Compositor II	

2 recto: p.3 Prologue Compositor II	7 verso: p.14 TEXT Compositor II	second sheet, replaced earlier setting
2 verso: p.4 Prologue Compositor II	7 recto: p.13 TEXT Compositor II	2 settings of inner forme

3 recto: p.5 Prologue end Compositor II	6 verso: p.12 TEXT Compositor II	third sheet, replaced earlier setting
3 verso: p.6 TEXT Compositor II	6 recto: p.11 TEXT Compositor II	2 settings of inner forme

4 recto: p.7 TEXT Compositor I	5 verso: p.10 TEXT Compositor I	inner sheet, not replaced
4 verso: p.8 blank	5 recto: p.9 TEXT Compositor II	

at speed, and on paper different from the rest of the book – could these sheets possibly replace earlier sheets? Could it be that they were finished as rapidly as the printers could manage just before the book was issued? In that case they would have been printed immediately after the completion of the final page of the book, where in a short epilogue Caxton courteously addressed the Prince of Wales 'now in his tendre iongth', and begged him to accept his work ' . . . of me his indigne serviteur'. Should that be the case, we have also to assume that the two sheets in the first quire replaced two sheets printed earlier on. They now contain the dedication and the beginning of the text of *Jason*. Why should two sheets have been replaced?

A positive answer to this last question is too much to be hoped for. But there is another factor that we can take into consideration; in the course of this investigation we have learned to distinguish two compositors, and we can recognize some of their habits. Most of *The History of Jason*, from leaf b 1 verso (page 18) on to the end, was set by only one compositor whom earlier on we have for this reason called the 'Jason compositor'. He is the compositor who tried to avoid the use of double *a*. In the first quire of *Jason* as it survives now the work was shared with the compositor whom we have seen at work in the early quartos and the *Canterbury Tales* (see Fig. 51). But the sheets that may have been reset were all set by the 'Jason compositor', who is likely to have done this simply in continuation of his long stint of work on this book. In the dedication his typesetting, notably the absence of double *a*'s, is entirely consistent. But in the opening pages of the text of *Jason* some inconsistencies have crept in, much as we have seen in the second set of quartos when he was copying work set by the first 'Canterbury Tales compositor'. We cannot be certain, but it is more than a mere guess if we now infer that in the text proper the 'Jason compositor' was copying five pages set by the 'Canterbury Tales compositor', and was – as before – occasionally influenced by his habits, but that in the new setting of the prologue (three pages) he set a text which had not been set before. In other words, there are indications that the prologue, containing the dedication, replaced an earlier one which does not survive. If this is correct, we must assume that some time during the printing of the book, before reaching the final page with the epilogue, Caxton had a reason for changing the prologue. And since the only purpose of the prologue was the dedication of the book, we may reasonably wonder whether the book was originally printed with a different dedicatee in mind. It is at this point (and only here) that we are entering into the realm of speculation.

It has always been a cause for some puzzlement that Caxton printed the *Recuyell* and *The History of Jason* with such a long time-gap between them. The two texts, both written by Raoul Lefèvre and both originally dedicated by the author to Philip the Good, Duke of Burgundy, are often found together, both in manuscript and in print. The *Recuyell*, as we have seen, was Caxton's first translation into English and he dedicated it to Margaret of York after she had commissioned the continuation of his translation. It was a highly appropriate text to translate for the young duchess. The legends of Troy and Hercules, the subject matter of the *Recuyell*, formed a substantial part in the complex legendary origins of the House of Burgundy which so preoccupied the dukes themselves as well as their literary entourage, and which reflect to a large extent their political aspirations. It is worthy of note that Caxton started his translation, as he informs the reader of his prologues, on 1 March 1468, when grandiose preparations were in full swing in Bruges for the celebration of the great Anglo-Burgundian alliance, the marriage of Charles the Bold and Margaret of York which was to take place in that city three months later.

It would have been natural if the *Recuyell* had then immediately been followed by the *Jason*, or even if the *Jason* had preceded it, as this is the order in which the texts customarily occur. *The History of Jason*, which relates the history of the Golden Fleece, is even more closely linked with Burgundian imagery than the Troy histories. The Order of the Golden Fleece, founded by Philip the Good, had become the symbol of Burgundian alliance. Jason was considered the ancestor, mythical but no less direct for that, of the Dukes of Burgundy. But even if Caxton translated the *Jason* in conjunction with his work on the *Recuyell* there was a delicate obstacle to dedicating it at once to Margaret of York. For listen how this story begins:

> Anciently the kynges and Princes of hye felicite were attendaunt and awayted whan their seed shold bringe forth generacion. But whan so was that they myghte not come therto. what prosperite they had Their lyf was traversid in contynuell bewailing, and they vysited temples and oracles vnto the consummacion of their dayes . . . (see Fig. 52).

Hardly words suitable for presentation to a bride, or later to a childless princess, the only hope of a dynasty deeply worried by the absence of a male heir. Words that had suddenly become acutely painful after 5 January 1477, when Charles the Bold fell before Nancy.

ANciently the kynges and Princes of hye felicite
Were attendaunt and awayted whan their seed
sholde bringe forth generacion. But whan so was
that they myghte not come therto, what prosperite they had
Their lyf was trauersid in contynuell bewailing, and
they vysited temples and oracles vnto the comsumacion
of their dayes, or vnto thenhaunsement of theyr orysons.
The noble kyng Eson of Myrmydone wherof is made men-
cion in the prologue, among alle other thinges & worldly
prosperitees was right nobly regnyng. Certes he had his
Royaume mayntened in pees, He had in mariage a right
fayr lady, but they were long to geder with oute hauyng
generacion, wherof their dayes were full of bewaylynges
and of litill playsir in the goodes of fortune. But they
were contynuelly in the temples and oracles. And no
thing of their desire befelle vnto them vnto the tyme that
the kyng began to fall and were old by aage. Thenne his
wyf conceyued of his seed and multeplied the generacion humayn of a right fayr sone At the burthe of this sone the noble quene deyde, And whan the kyng Eson sawe
his wyf so departe from lyf to deth, he bewepte her long
tyme and made her obsequye Right solempnly. And after he reioyed in his sone newe born. whom he named Jason ¶ Jason thenne grewe in beaulte merueillously, in so
moche that his fader the kyng Eson toke grete playsir to
nourisshe hym. The tyme passid Jason grewe so long that
he coud goo and speke. And the noble kyng his fader be-
cam auncient in suche manere that he myght no more helpe
hym self. And on a daye callid Jason his sone and sayd

52. The beginning of the text of *The History of Jason* in Caxton's translation.
British Library, C.10.b.3, leaf [a] 5 recto.

Caxton: a merchant of printed books

Historians must speculate. This is one of the reasons why we must at this point part with the analogy of the courtroom – it becomes too limiting. Ultimately we have a different purpose: not to judge the past and its investigators but to understand them. In order to achieve this we can start with examining material objects, and obtain from them as much evidence as we know how to; but it would be naive to assume that the past has left us enough material to allow a perfect reconstruction based on tangible facts alone. We have to fill in gaps, and provide tentative links. Newly established facts inevitably lead to new areas of speculation.

In the investigation of Caxton's early books we were concentrating on a restricted field. Even so we have met other historical disciplines: palaeography, textual and literary history, and the political history of England and of Burgundy. The specialisation inherent in the development of modern scholarship is apt to make each subject an end in itself. In consequence there is a growing reluctance, even a fear, to use the results of studies in related fields. Branches of scholarship become isolated, and bibliography is no exception. Thus, having presented the facts and completed our investigation we must assess the relationship of this study to other disciplines, both those which we have used and those to which this work is of potential use. Does it relate to other historical studies? Could our findings affect the view of the introduction of printing into England held in other fields of historical research?

The arrival of the printing press in England did not change the course of political history. Printing was not used as a political instrument in England until later. There may have been an immediate impact on religious life, since we have established that Caxton soon produced a substantial liturgical work, the *Ordinale*. Probably the first attempt to influence ecclesiastical events by producing a document in print was Caxton's printing of the *Officium visitationis beate Mariae Virginis* in 1480. Caxton must have been commissioned to print these and also similar works; it is likely that this was another form of patronage to which we cannot attach a name.

Caxton's relations with his named patrons have become clearer, and this brings us to literary history, and the history of publishing. In the case of Earl Rivers the connexion lasted long, and had a greater influence on Caxton's publications than has been thought so far. Here was a man with a literary taste more refined than Caxton's own. It was a relationship that subsisted on more than patronage alone, for there are signs here of the normal, ultimately beneficial tension between author and publisher.

100

But for a full understanding of the newly ascertained fact that Caxton's first major book in England was the *Canterbury Tales* we have to think in a context of the book trade rather than of literary history. Through choosing this most English of texts, a bestseller to the present day, Caxton gave himself the best possible chance of persuading an English public, not used to such a thing, to buy books.

Caxton's long experience of life in the southern Netherlands, in Flanders and in Brabant, is significant. There he had come to know a reading public spread among far more layers of society than in England and most other countries at that time. In Flanders and Brabant owners of substantial libraries could be found among the secular clergy, the professional classes, merchants and administrators, as well as more exalted circles, with a highly developed book-culture. It is among the merchants and officials of this area that Caxton must have acquired his taste for books, a taste that he was happily to share later with his countrymen, to whom it was new. His desire to impart to others what he had learned on the Continent is amply apparent from Caxton's many translations into English of works new to an English public. But the fact that in Westminster the publication of the indigenous *Canterbury Tales* preceded any translation, highlights a preference that was to set a pattern for a long time to come. English printing was *English*. Printers in England did not print books that could be obtained from overseas through the channels of the book trade. A flood of printed material was imported from the Continent through the trade in the decades after 1480. In comparison the output of the presses active in England was insignificant in quantity. The importation of books in Latin is recorded from 1477 on, soon after Caxton's arrival. From then on the printing press made as much of an impact on every level of intellectual life in England as it did elsewhere, but this was not through the English presses but through the import trade, in which Caxton himself participated. However, English printers did produce texts which could not be obtained elsewhere. Only rarely did imported books cover the same ground or affect the same aspects of life. This gave English printing a unique national and almost chauvinistic character.

Caxton seems to have foreseen this from the beginning, and to have turned deliberately to what the Continent could not provide ready-made. When he settled in Westminster he must have planned to begin an independent press, and to publish literary works in English – texts that were his own delight – for a public that was not accustomed to owning books. Patrons, royal or otherwise, were a matter of opportunity and not a basis for business. To prepare the way for the *Canterbury Tales* he printed some appetising little books which could be assembled to a sizeable volume. Originally courtly

101

poetry, these texts now began to appeal to the aspiring classes in England. Caxton gave these books a form in print that must have made it easy to win over a wide readership. The continuation of his career in England, with a steady succession of books aimed at the same kind of public, shows that this course had been succesful. He had made readers.

Sources and literature

Early literature on English printing:

Most early literature on printing in England can be found in chronological arrangement, with notes, in Walter L. Heilbronner, *Printing and the book in fifteenth-century England: a bibliographical survey,* Charlottesville, The Bibliographical Society of the University of Virginia, 1967. An exhibition held in 1976 at the St. Bride Printing Library entitled *Caxtoniana, or the progress of Caxton studies from the earliest times to 1976* illustrated many of the highlights of Caxton studies.

Printing at Oxford:

The printer's copy used for the first book printed in Oxford was investigated after Dr A. C. de la Mare had discovered that the manuscript British Library, MS Sloane 1579 had been used for this purpose. She revealed this in *The Times Literary Supplement* of 24 March 1978, p. 364. For a fuller study see A. C. de la Mare and Lotte Hellinga, 'The first book printed in Oxford: the *Expositio Symboli* of Rufinus', in *Transactions of the Cambridge Bibliographical Society* 7, pt. 2, 1978, pp. 184–244.

Book collecting in the eighteenth century:

For English book collectors in the eighteenth century see the relevant section in: Seymour de Ricci, *English collectors of books and manuscripts (1530–1930) and their marks of ownership,* Cambridge, 1930. The same author has devoted a monograph to the collecting of Caxtons: Seymour de Ricci, *A census of Caxtons,* Oxford, The Bibliographical Society Illustrated Monographs No xv, 1909. Auction catalogues are an important source of knowledge for the study of book collecting and for tracing the history of individual copies. An invaluable research tool is A. N. L. Munby and Lenore Coral, *British book sale catalogues 1676–1800: a union list,* London, 1977.

Dates in *The Recuyell of the Historyes of Troye*:

Caxton's own prologues and epilogues were first collected and edited by W. J. B. Crotch, *The prologues and epilogues of William Caxton,* London, Early English Text Society, Original Series No 176, 1928. They have later been edited again by N. F. Blake, *Caxton's own prose,* London, 1973.

Dates as given in the fifteenth century can present problems, since one cannot always be certain which year style was followed; the beginning of the year could be reckoned from the first day of January, but also from Christmas Day, Easter, or Lady Day (25 March). In the Netherlands the practice varied from one chancery to another, but the bourgeoisie would commonly follow the year style in which the year began on 1 January. See R. Fruin, *Handboek der chronologie voornamelijk van Nederland,* Alphen aan de Rijn, 1934, p.55, 57–122. Dates given by printers in books printed in the Netherlands are almost invariably reckoned from 1 January. In the interpretation of the dates given by Caxton in the *Recuyell* I have therefore assumed that he followed the practice common in the country where he had lived by then for 25 years. This is borne out by his dating of *The Game of Chess,* see p. 48. In England, however, the year was more often reckoned from Lady Day, although not all printers in England always followed this practice.

William Blades' work on Caxton was well documented in the exhibition *Caxtoniana*, held at the St. Bride Printing Library in 1976, which was mentioned above. See also: Robin Myers, 'William Blades's debt to Henry Bradshaw and G. I. F. Tupper in his Caxton studies: a further look at unpublished documents', in *The Library*, 5th ser., 33, 1978, pp. 265–283. For the lithographer G. I. F. Tupper see: Robin Myers, 'George Isaac Frederick Tupper, facsimilist, "whose ability in this description of work is beyond praise" (1820–1911)' in *Transactions of the Cambridge Bibliographical Society* 7, pt. 2, 1978, pp. 113–134.
For the development of the modern study of incunabula by Henry Bradshaw and Jan Willem Holtrop see: W. and L. Hellinga, *Henry Bradshaw's correspondence on incunabula with J. W. Holtrop and M. F. A. G. Campbell*, 2 vols., Amsterdam, 1968, 1978.
The crowning glory of Blades' career, the Caxton exhibition, is recorded in the catalogue entitled: *Caxton celebrations 1877: Catalogue of the loan collection of antiquities, curiosities and appliances connected with the art of printing*, London, 1877. Blades used a copy of this catalogue as the basis for an eight-volume collection of memorabilia concerning the preparation of the exhibition. It is now in the British Library, press-mark C. 61. c. 8.
The stained glass window illustrated on the cover of the present book was described in *A history and description of the Caxton Memorial Window in St Margaret's Church, Westminster, with a list of the Subscribers and Committee and the full text of the sermon preached at the unveiling of the window by the Rev. Canon Farrar, D. D, April 30th, 1882*, London, 1882. The window was erected by public subscription, mainly from printers and publishers. It was damaged during the Second World War.

THE CAXTON CELEBRATIONS IN 1976: THE LEASE OF 1476 AND THE INDULGENCE

E. Gordon Duff, *Fifteenth-century English books: a bibliography of books and documents printed in England and of books for the English market printed abroad*. Oxford, The Bibliographical Society Illustrated Monographs No XVIII, 1917. Duff largely agreed with Blades' chronological arrangement, but sometimes showed greater caution. He mentioned the Westminster lease in *William Caxton*, Chicago, 1905, p. 33. The *shopa* got no mention in his *The printers, stationers and bookbinders of Westminster and London from 1476 to 1535*, Cambridge, 1906, which was published later than his *William Caxton*, but in which the section dealing with the period before 1501 was based on the author's Sandars lectures delivered in 1899. The text of the document was partly published by W. J. B. Crotch, *The prologues and epilogues of William Caxton*, London, Early English Text Society, Original Series No 176, 1928, pp. clii-clvii. This edition has unfortunately proved to be not impeccable. Mr Howard M. Nixon first put forward his review of the known facts in his notes to the exhibition in Westminster Abbey Library which was opened after the celebration in commemoration of the introduction of printing into England in the Abbey on 20 September 1976. Nixon published his observations in 'Caxton, his contemporaries and successors in the book trade from Westminster documents' in *The Library*, 5th ser., 31, 1976, pp. 305–326.
The Indulgence of 1476 had been discovered in the Public Record Office by S. C. Ratcliff. The find was first made public in *The Times* of 7 February 1928 by Alfred W. Pollard who subsequently gave an extensive description followed by a discussion of the implications of the find in 'The new Caxton Indulgence', in *The Library*, 4th ser., 9, 1928, pp. 86–89 (with facsimile).

A bibliography of research in the years between 1877 and 1967 is found in chronological arrangement in Walter L. Heilbronner, *Printing and the book in fifteenth-century England: a bibliographical survey*. Charlottesville, The Bibliographical Society of the University of Virginia, 1967. This can usefully be supplemented by *The new Cambridge bibliography of English Literature* vol. I, ed. G. Watson, Cambridge, 1974, in particular the sections 'Printing and bookselling' (941–1006) and 'William Caxton' (667–674). Literature published from the year 1890 is listed in: T. H. Howard-Hill, *British bibliography and textual criticism: a bibliography*, Oxford, 1979, vol. IV, Nos. 4218–4350a (William Caxton). Of the recent biographies of Caxton the most important are: Norman F. Blake, *Caxton and his world*, London, 1969. George D. Painter, *William Caxton: a quincentenary biography of England's first printer*, London, 1976. Norman F. Blake, *Caxton: England's first publisher*, London, 1976. They contain valuable reading lists.

The studies mentioned in particular in the text were published as follows: George D. Painter, 'Caxton through the looking glass. An enquiry into the offsets on a fragment of Caxton's Fifteen Oes, with a census of Caxton binding', in *Gutenberg-Jahrbuch 1963*, pp. 73–88.

José Ruysschaert, 'Les manuscrits autographes de deux oeuvres de Lorenzo Guglielmo Traversagni imprimées chez Caxton', in *Bulletin of The John Rylands Library Manchester* 36, 1953–4, pp. 191–197.

Colonel Birch first published his discovery of the Cologne records in *The Times Literary Supplement* of 5 April 1924, p. 232. It was subsequently published fully as J. G. Birch, 'William Caxton's stay at Cologne' in *The Library*, 4th ser., 4, 1924, pp. 50–52.

Caxton's stay at Cologne was much illuminated by Severin Corsten, 'Caxton in Cologne', in: *Papers presented to the Caxton International Congress 1976: Journal of the Printing Historical Society* 11, 1976–7, pp. 1–18.

The most recent discussion of the date of *The Game of Chess* is by Norman F. Blake, 'Dating the first book printed in English', in *Gutenberg-Jahrbuch 1978*, pp. 43–50.

It took a long time to understand that Johannes Veldener was an important figure behind Caxton's typography. Most of the literature developing this was discussed by Painter in his biography of Caxton and by Corsten in his contribution to the Caxton Congress (see above). Veldener is also considered as a major influence by Nicolas Barker, 'Caxton's Typography', in *Papers presented to the Caxton International Congress: Journal of the Printing Historical Society* 11, 1976–7, pp. 114–133.

PRESENT RESEARCH FOR THE CATALOGUE OF INCUNABULA IN THE BRITISH LIBRARY

Researches discussed in this section were all carried out in preparation of the volume 'England' of BMC. Full bibliographical details of the catalogue are: *Catalogue of books printed in the XVth Century now in the British Museum*, parts i–x, London 1908–1970 (parts i–viii reprinted with additional notes, London, 1962; part ix reprinted with additional notes, London, 1967).

As the second section of this book concentrates entirely on recent work, not every argument that has been put forward in the past, and which must now be considered as supporting evidence for the arguments based on typographical evidence and paper research has been given consideration here. Thus it has been observed that the *Ordinale* and its Advertisement have uneven line endings, and that it must therefore belong to an early period of Caxton's Westminster printing, certainly not later than 1479 (G. D. Painter, *William Caxton*, p. 98). The words of Robert Copland who may have been an apprentice of Caxton, written in the preface to his *Apollonius of Tyre* (1510) have often been quoted as an indication that Caxton started with printing small books before attempting a major work in Westminster. They are open to several interpretations (see G. D. Painter, *William Caxton*, p. 84).

The chronology of Caxton's early Westminster books which is put forward in the present study was first made public in the BBC television programme, *The Printer's Tale*, presented by Paul Needham and myself, in the series 'Discoveries' produced by Derrick Amoore and Ron Johnston, broadcast on 12 April 1980. The paper evidence was discussed by Paul Needham, in 'Bibliographical evidence from the paper stocks of English incunabula', in *Buch und Text im 15. Jahrhundert/Book and Text in the fifteenth century: Proceedings of a conference held in the Herzog August Bibliothek Wolfenbüttel March 1–3, 1978*, Hamburg, 1981. An extensive study by Paul Needham with full discussion of the paper evidence is in preparation. C. F. Bühler's textual arguments for the priority of the Pierpont Morgan Library's *The Churl and the Bird* were published in *The Library*, 4th ser., 21, 1941, pp. 279–284.

The figure of Johannes Veldener in connexion with printing in the Netherlands, as well as the spread of Caxton's Type 3 and its use by other printers was discussed by Wytze and Lotte Hellinga, *The fifteenth-century printing types of the Low Countries*, Amsterdam, 1966. For the spread of Caxton Type 3 see vol. I, pp. 24, 49, 66 and vol. II, Plates 61–64. The use of Caxton's Type 3 by some of his contemporaries in England was investigated by W. J. Partridge, 'The use of Caxton's Type 3 by John Lettou and William de Machlinia,' in *The British Library Journal* (forthcoming).

The textual arguments for the relation of the various versions of the *Dictes* are based on those put forward in the discussion (which remained inconclusive) between C. F. Bühler and G. Legman. Those of Dr Bühler are now collected in *Early books and manuscripts. Forty years of research by Curt F. Bühler*, New York, 1973, pp. 3–33; his opponent's views are found in G. Legman, 'A word on Caxton's Dictes', in *The Library*, 5th ser., 3, 1949, pp. 155–185.

The investigation of the early history of the Malory Manuscript was first published by Lotte Hellinga and Hilton Kelliher, 'The Malory Manuscript', in *The British Library Journal* 3, 1977, pp. 91–113. Revised versions of the contributions of both authors were published in: Hilton Kelliher, 'The early history of the Malory Manuscript', and Lotte Hellinga, 'The Malory Manuscript and Caxton', in *Aspects of Malory*, edited by Toshiyuki Takamiya and Derek Brewer, Woodbridge, Arthurian Studies I, 1981, pp. 143–158, 127–141. Professor R. M. Lumiansky, New York, kindly brought to my attention the error in Caxton's casting off and setting which is quoted here.

The variant settings of *The History of Jason* were noted by C. F. Bühler, 'Caxton's History of Jason', in *Papers of the Bibliographical Society of America* 34, 1940, pp. 254–261.

CAXTON AND THE BOOK TRADE

Caxton's direct involvement with the trade in printed books was first shown by Nellie J. M. Kerling, 'Caxton and the trade in printed books', in *The Book Collector* 4, 1955, pp. 190–199. A more general discussion of the book trade in England is found in Graham Pollard, 'The English market for printed books' in *Publishing History* 4, 1978, pp. 9–48, and in Elizabeth Armstrong, 'English purchases of printed books from the Continent 1465–1526', in *The English Historical Review* 94, 1979, pp. 268–290. Book ownership in the Low Countries and Caxton's relation to it was discussed by Lotte Hellinga, 'Caxton and the bibliophiles', in *Actes du XIe Congrès International de Bibliophilie*, Brussels, 1981, pp. 11–38.

Index